ABOUT THE WHITE PAPERS

Dating back to 18th Century England, White Papers have long provided a forum for exploring important social and political issues.

The farmers, chefs, food writers, academics and other experts presented here have extended the tradition a step further by translating the concept of sustainable cuisine into practical food choices.

This "food for thought" was published on the occasion of a Sustainable Cuisine Dinner ("food from the kitchen") commemorating the last Earth Day of this Century. The event, hosted by the Earth Pledge Foundation and the Earth Communications Office on April 22nd, 1999 took place at the Carriage House, a national landmark in New York City.

Ten chefs offered their interpretation of sustainable cuisine with a menu that included rare cheeses, fresh vegetables, exotic fish, organic wines, beers, chocolate and more.

Earth Pledge and ECO acknowledge the significant contribution each chef made to our exploration of sustainable cuisine.

We offer a special acknowledgment to team leader Jeffrey Mora, not only for his cooking, but also for his tireless efforts and ability to make the impossible—coordinating a dinner with chefs from California, Florida, Louisiana, New Jersey, New York, Pennsylvania and overseas in Holland—possible.

1999 Earth Day Sustainable Cuisine Dinner Chefs Team

Peter Berley
Angelica Kitchen, New York City

Alfonso Contrisciani
Opus 251 & Circa, Philadelphia

Keith Keogh
California Culinary Academy, San Francisco

Norman Love
Ritz Carlton, Naples, Florida

Rick Moonen
Oceana Restaurant, New York City

Jeffrey Mora
Metropolitan Culinary Services, Los Angeles

Michel Nischan
Heartbeat, W New York, New York City

Paul Prudhomme
K. Paul's Louisiana Kitchen, New Orleans

Cas Spijkers
The Swaen Hotel, Oisterwisk, Holland

Tom Vaccaro
Trump Hotels & Casino Resorts, Atlantic City, New Jersey

earthpledgefoundation

Promoting Sustainability Since 1991

The Earth Pledge Foundation is a non-profit communications company that produces projects with the private sector to advance the concept of sustainable development—our need to live and work in a prosperous and healthy environment. The Foundation's mission highlights the interconnectedness of art, architecture, technology, democracy, food, tourism, media and the environment. Working with our partners, sponsors and clients, Earth Pledge makes sustainability accessible through print, new media, special events, educational programs, community and public relations, marketing and strategic planning.

TABLE OF CONTENTS

Sustainable Cuisine White Papers are part of the Earth Pledge Foundation Series on
Sustainable Development. Copyright ©1999 Earth Pledge Foundation. All rights reserved.
Material in this publication may not be reproduced in any form without permission from
the publisher. Earth Pledge Foundation, 149 East 38th Street, New York, NY 10016.
Telephone (212) 573-6968. www.earthpledge.org. President: Theodore W. Kheel,
Publisher: Leslie Hoffman, Editor: JP Frenza, Art Director: Kristen Kiger, Assistant:
Meredith Sparrow.

Second printing February, 2000. Project Manager: Mindy Fox.

Printed on 100% recycled paper, 25% hemp and 75% post-consumer waste using
environmentally responsible techniques.

Introduction

Leslie Hoffman, Executive Director

Earth Pledge has been on the trail of sustainable cuisine since 1995 when Ted Kheel and I had met for lunch to plan our First Caribbean Conference on Sustainable Tourism. We were about to invite a diverse group of thought leaders, hoteliers, government and industry representatives to consider the benefits of sustainability for the Caribbean basin.

In response to seeing what he wanted to eat for lunch listed as Spa Cuisine on the menu, Ted grimaced. Not being one to respond easily to "eat it, it's good for you," he looked over with a creative sparkle in his eyes and said, "What do you think about sustainable cuisine?" The obvious answer to that question set us in motion.

We included the subject at the Caribbean Conference and then followed up in February of 1996 with a Sustainable Cuisine Dinner at the United Nations honoring our friend and supporter, the artist Robert Rauschenberg. Michael Romano of the famed Union Square Cafe led ten nationally renowned chefs in preparing the dinner. The enthusiastic response to sustainable cuisine led us to conclude that we were on to something big.

Sometime in 1997 we asked the great restaurateur Joe Baum if he would join us in promoting sustainable cuisine. He pondered thoughtfully and became an ardent advocate. Joe's death in the Fall of '98 was an enormous loss in many respects.

Joe and I had agreed to host a Sustainable Cuisine Dinner at Windows on the World for The New School conference *Food: Nature and Culture* in November. The Dinner was ultimately hosted by Jonathan Fanton, President of The New School, and Earth Pledge at a warm and intimate gathering in Mr. Fanton's home.

Exposure to the concept of sustainable cuisine can empower anyone engaging in the production, distribution, preparation or consumption of food. It has become clear that anybody with the desire can respond to it and translate it into a meaningful part of their daily activities. This is an idea that resonates with our time, our place and the very essence of what it is to be human. We need this. So I call on all of you to use it and pass it on.

Preface

Paul Newman

When thinking about food, and being asked to write the preface to this collection of White Papers, it occurred to me that sustainable cuisine is the Viagra of life.

There are a cornucopia of dreams. Sensual dreams, underwater dreams, frustration dreams. And then there is food. Food and the pleasure we derive from it sustains us. It arrives from our understanding of how to prepare, present and distribute it.

My long time friend, A.E. Hotchner, and I filled old wine bottles with salad dressing to give away at Christmas. Our reason for formulating Newman's Own was that if it was good enough for our pals, it was good enough for the public.

We never dreamed that what began as a gesture of goodwill amongst family and friends at Christmas would turn into a most powerful venture. This holiday offering became $100 million in after tax dollars donated to charitable and educational causes.

It is our belief that eating and living well is the best revenge. To create cuisine is to sustain life. Food should be simple, imaginative, digestible, and healthy. It should be good for our bodies, good for our minds, and enrich the soul.

Sustainable cuisine's message is to ensure that food and its processes are held to the highest standards so that, in the end, we do not harm the environment and we protect our future. This message is fundamental to all of us and to the generations to follow. These White Papers clearly express the importance of our need to re-think our approach, and I commend and support their efforts.

Know the Source

Diane Bowen

California Certified Organic Farmers (CCOF)
1115 Mission Street
Santa Cruz, CA 95060
www.ccof.org

❧

"The further we are from a state of nature, the more we lose our natural tastes."

—*Rousseau*

It will soon be the high season at our local farmers' market—the time of year when I know the growers of much of the food I eat—and I know them personally. In fact, I've been to many of their farms. I often see their farms in my mind's eye as I prepare the salad or the potatoes for an evening meal. Envisioning the farm and the farmer adds to my enjoyment of preparing and eating organically grown food.

While there is no organic standard for linking the farm with the consumer, doing so has long been a cherished ideal within the organic community. This is a key incentive in the burgeoning system of Community Supported Agriculture. People who share the farmer's investment, and farmers who share their bounty with investors in their farming season create a powerful linkage of food with its source. The ultimate linkage is growing one's own.

Farmers' markets can provide opportunities for people to know the source of their food. But sometimes there are missed opportunities. If the farmer herself is not present, activity is too brisk to allow for conversation, and printed materials are unavailable, the connection between the buyer and his food source may be limited to the direct exchange of money and goods, rather than of information.

At the retail level, the direct link between farmer and consumer is unavailable. However some California Certified Organic Farmers (CCOF) members have creatively addressed this challenge through information services and packaging. Produce distributor, Veritable Vegetable, regularly includes farm profiles in its retailer newsletter. These profiles end up as laminated posters in the produce section or articles in a retailer's newsletter to customers. Lundberg Family Farms have mastered the use of their package itself to convey farm images and information. The image of the four Lundberg brothers "out standing" in their rice field sends a positive message. Over the past seven years, Pavich Family Farms has produced a newsletter, which is directly mailed to over 5,000 consumers. It features a full range of information, from organic farming methods to favorite family recipes. Individuals are invited to join the mailing list by calling, writing, or subscribing via the Pavich Family Farms' Web site. Web sites are now providing a promising and powerful tool to help people know their food source. In contrast to the small space taken up by a Web site address on a package, the amount of information a Web site can provide is voluminous.

I believe that there is a great potential for organic food processors and other re-packers of organic foods to increase sales by providing more information about where, how and by whom the package's ingredients were grown. While not every farm source can be featured in packaging or point-of-purchase materials, selected farms might be. The benefit of consumer preference and loyalty vis-a-vis the competition may outweigh the apparent cost to the processor of revealing their ingredient sources. Inspiring images have long been used to market consumer goods. Billions of boxes of Wheaties have been sold with images of celebrity athletes. Why not sell billions of boxes of organic cereal with images of farmers who grew what's inside?

Retailers have a valuable role to play in building growth in the organic trade. In most cases, they are the direct link to the consumer. They can buy produce direct from the farmer and work with the farmer to develop point-of-sale information. They can display and distribute materials provided by their organic distributor or organic non-profit associations. They can ask manufacturers and re-packers to include information about where, how, and by whom the product's ingredients were grown. Organic restaurants can also distinguish themselves and increase customer loyalty by letting their customers know about the source of their meal.

Restaurants can also link farming to the dining experience. Restaurants that utilize organic foods in their menu items will serve themselves and their customers well by providing information about the source of organic ingredients. This will enrich the culinary experience and build customer loyalty.

We are in a period of rampant growth and globalization of the organic foods business. Many of us share a concern about the organic food system becoming as bland and depersonalized as the conventional food system is now. While organic food may also travel many miles through multiple levels of food distribution, information about how that food was grown can travel with it. It's up to us in the system — organic farmers, distributors, manufacturers, retailers, restaurateurs and non-profit associations — to keep the good news about organic farming flowing, and preserve the cherished idea that organic means not only a way of farming, but also valuable information about how one's food was grown.

Understanding Organic Farming

Gene Kahn, CEO

Cascadian Farms
719 Metcalf Street
Sedro-Wolley, WA 98284
www.cfarm.com

❧

Biodiversity—short for biological diversity—is perhaps most commonly defined as "the full variety of life on earth." Some circles use the metaphor "Web of Life" to highlight the interconnectedness and fragility of all living things. Many people don't think of farming, especially large-scale farming, as having a variety of flora and fauna or being connected to biodiversity. In fact, it is common for many people to associate biodiversity more with the rainforest than with the wheat farmer in Iowa or the strawberry grower in California.

But in fact, farming does have a relationship to biodiversity and the health of ecosystems, on a scale both small and grand.

"Whether pesticides are applied by one person with a hand-powered sprayer to individual plants or by a crop-dusting airplane over many square kilometers, much of the associated biodiversity is reduced," states Catherine Badgley in the article "Can Agriculture and Biodiversity Exist?" in the Fall 1998 issue of Wild Earth magazine.

As World War II ended, a new relationship blossomed between conventional agriculture and the chemical industry. Astonishing increases in food production occurred after synthetic fertilizers and pesticides, developed for war use, were applied at home to increase crop yield, control ripening time, meet quality and cosmetic standards, and prolong shelf life. There was little concern regarding possible human, ecological or environmental hazards. In 1962, publication of Rachel Carson's groundbreaking book, *Silent Spring*, focused attention on these issues. Even so, pesticide use has increased and newer pesticides, more potent than ever, pose continued threats to the environment, humans and wildlife.

For example, a study released in October 1998 reports the results of a survey of frog and toad populations in agricultural areas in the St. Lawrence Valley, Canada. Researchers compared amphibians that live in agricultural areas where pesticides are applied regularly to those that live in areas where little pesticide use had occurred. Many of the frogs in the agricultural areas had extra legs growing from their stomachs and backs; other frogs had only stumps for hind legs or fused hind legs. After observing nearly 30,000 frogs and toads, they determined that the incidence of limb deformities in frogs in agricultural areas was nearly seven times greater than those living in non-agricultural areas.

All along the food chain, from tiny microbes in the soil to fish in streams and large mammals in the wild, scientists have demonstrated how pesticides used in conventional agricultural practices have a profoundly negative impact on nature's fragile balance. "We know that there has been considerable environmental pollution by persistent pesticides, particularly in the last four decades, and that residues occur widely in soil, in water and also in most of the biota (flora and fauna)," states Clive Edwards, professor of Entomology at Ohio State University, in his study *The Fate of Pesticides in the Environment.*

Protecting biodiversity means ensuring the conservation of species, ecosystems and gene pools so essential ecological processes and life-support systems are maintained for future generations. Organic farmers have a commitment to ecologically sustainable farming methods that strive for a balance with nature.

Organic farmers use integrated, lower-impact approaches to managing crops and the soil, rather than using synthetic pesticides or fertilizers. Techniques include:

- Rotating crops grown in each field over several years, rather than growing only one or two crops in short rotations.

- Establishing cover crops such as legumes to supply nutrients to the soil, rather than using synthetic fertilizers which often damage soil quality and reduce the biological diversity of the soil. Cover crops also reduce soil erosion from water and wind.

- Adding composts to the soil to build nutrient availability and improve soil biological functions.

- Enhancing biodiversity helps promote biological control of pests and diseases.

- Augmenting and encouraging on-farm natural refuges for fauna and flora promotes a more diverse and healthy ecosystem.

- Soil-building programs (e.g., compost applications, cover crops, reduced tillage) support habitats for macro and micro-organisms that perform beneficial functions for plant roots.

Cascadian's Home Farm is an example of our commitment to the environment and a healthy ecosystem. Sound organic farming practices and nourishing relationships between plants, insects and animals allow our crops to be grown without the use of synthetic pesticides. Farm managers Jim and Harlyn Meyer have put up wooden boxes that encourage the nesting of mason bees, which are needed to pollinate the farm's blueberry bushes. Fruit and vegetable crops are rotated each season to maintain the soil's health. Compost is made from grass pasture and sawdust from a local mill. The 75 acres of old-growth forests surrounding the Home Farm have been preserved and provide refuge to bald eagles.

Our mission at Cascadian Farm is to break the cycle of environmental destruction that can be a consequence of certain conventional agricultural practices. Through our dedication to organic agriculture, we work to protect the intricate balance of all living things on Earth. And we think that's important for preserving today's resources for tomorrow's generations.

Sustainable Cuisine on the Vine

Chartrand Imports

P.O. Box 1319
Rockland, Maine 04841
www.midcoast.com/~chartran

᠃᠊

Chartrand Imports began importing organically grown French wines to the US in 1985—in fact, it was the first American company to import and sell a line of organic wines here.

Paul Chartrand, owner and founder, worked in the natural foods and the organic farming movement after studying chemical engineering at Columbia University. He discovered many wonderful wines made by organic growers during a trip in 1982 while working as an apprentice on French organic farms and vineyards.

We only sell wines that are certified organically grown by independent third party verification. In France there are three such organizations with basically the same standards: Ecocert, Qualité France and Bio Contact. Terre et Vie, and UNIA.

In Italy the process is certified by AIAB. They all work by standards approved by their Ministry of Agriculture for the sale of foods as organically grown, or *biologique*.

Organic wines are produced using only organically grown grapes. Synthetic fertilizers or pesticides are not allowed on the vines or in the soil. Strict rules also govern the winemaking process and storage conditions. Many substances used to stabilize or to assist wine to be more palatable are avoided by organic growers. Only pure sulfur dioxide is used as an antioxidant, and amounts allowed are far less than common usage in Europe or the US. This sulfite has been used for centuries in winemaking. Without the harmless treatment, a winemaker risks producing an inconsistent or extremely fragile wine. We offer several wines that are made with no added sulfur, in addition to our full line of organic, low sulfite wines.

Many persons find organic wines to be more easily drinkable and more flavorful than wines made by more industrial standards. The healthy soil contributes to a rich and full flavored wine, in balance and requiring no extra additives. In addition we are supporting farmers who preserve their soil and their communities by avoiding the many pesticides commonly used on grapes. Such winemakers are proud of their craft and their wines.

Sustainable Food Systems

Jennifer L. Wilkins, PhD, RD,
Senior Extension Associate

Division of Nutritional Sciences
College of Agriculture and Life Sciences
Cornell University
Ithaca, NY 14850-4401

❧

S ustainable cuisine is a pattern of eating that derives from a sustainable food system and supports the goals of such a system. Sustainable cuisine is a way of eating that ensures rather than compromises the ability of future generations to enjoy an abundant, nourishing, wholesome, flavorful and safe food supply.

There are several potential goals of a sustainable food system:

- *Nourishment and food security.* First, the primary goal of any food system is nourishment. In a sustainable food system, food will be available and accessible to all persons through local non-emergency sources.

- *Self-reliance.* Sustainable food systems require that communities or regions achieve a degree of self-reliance in food, and explore the extent to which they can and should meet their own food needs.

- *Direct product/consumer links.* In a sustainable food system, opportunities for consumers and producers to interact directly during transactions around food would be commonplace.

- *Maximal participation and business generation.* Within a particular region, more food businesses would be established thus allowing more people to find employment in various segments of the food system.

- *Abundant natural and social capital.* Sustainable community food systems can also protect and regenerate natural resources and build social capital.

- *Optimal amount of farmland, farms, and farmers.* Clearly, no food system will be sustainable if land is not preserved for farming, if smaller farms aren't viable, and if farming isn't perceived as an economically attractive vocation for men and women.

- *Diversity, variability and decentralization.* Diversity, variability and decentralization would be the pervasive tendencies, as opposed to the specialization, standardization and centralization that typifies much of the current global food system.

- *Socially just.* The manner in which our food is produced and moves from field to table would be socially just.

- *Cause-based not symptom-based solutions.* The search for solutions to the inevitable problems in the food system (such as pests in the farmers' fields and food insecurity in our communities) would focus on the causes of these problems (mono-cropping in the case of pests; lack of jobs and competitively priced food, and absence of competitively priced food stores in the case of food insecurity).

- *Rational public policies.* Food and agriculture policies would ensure the sustainability of the food system by encouraging ecological farming practices and processing methods, decreasing barriers to local marketing, and embedding links to local agriculture in federal food assistance programs.

Based on these goals, a sustainable cuisine would feature foods that were grown in environmentally responsible ways. Foods would be processed, marketed, and consumed as close as possible to the farms on which it was grown. This cuisine would emphasize whole foods, minimally processed and packaged, and would be seasonally varied in accordance with the nearby agricultural production. Sustainable cuisine would not eliminate but treat as special items out-of-season imports and imports of food items that cannot be grown in the region. A sustainable cuisine would be a celebration of the agricultural potential of the place in which it is promoted. It would be in keeping with the US Dietary Guidelines and existing data on natural resource requirements for production of different commodities. Therefore, a sustainable cuisine would not necessarily eliminate animal products but be predominantly plant-based, incorporating animal products in a prudent manner and reflecting the essential role animals play in integrated farming systems.

There is tremendous need for and an absolute inevitability regarding a sustainable cuisine. Indications of unsustainability in the agriculture and food system are numerous. Many believe that human population growth and resource use have exceeded natural carrying capacity. By considering the natural resources (both local and global) used to feed a population, the ecological impact of keeping different groups of humans fed would be more evident. This is critical in order to determine long-term sustainability in our agriculture and food systems.

In daily life, individuals would consider where their food comes from and endeavor year around to choose foods (fresh, stored and processed) that are or could be grown on farms in their local region. Individuals would also de-emphasize highly processed and packed foods and emphasize whole foods in their plant-based diets.

How does sustainable cuisine affect our College?

Consumers are largely unaware of the local and global environmental, social and economic impacts of their daily food choices. Information on these impacts is not incorporated in most nutrition education strategies and is not part of food labeling. We have

supported several efforts to increase consumer awareness of how eating locally and seasonally can support
the local food and agriculture system. The Agriculture
Experiment Station and Cornell Cooperative
Extension supports several research and extension
programs that encourage sustainable food systems.

Our Division supported the Northeast Regional
Food Guide, based on the US Dietary Guidelines
for Americans, plus additional guidelines to promote
foods grown and processed in the northeast region:

- Choose a Diet With Plenty of Foods Produced in
  the Northeast.

- Eat a Seasonally Varied Diet—Especially Fruits
  and Vegetables.

Sustainable cuisine has the potential to build a
tremendous sense of community by connecting eaters
and growers. Eating seasonally and locally, and pur-
posefully minimizing deleterious affects of their food
choices will heighten citizens' sense of participation
in and responsibility for the future of the food system.
Obviously, if the goals of a sustainable food system are
to be achieved, much social change will be required.

—⋙⋘—

A Philosophy of Food and Cooking

Tim Ryan

Education Division
The Culinary Institute of America
433 Albany Post Road
Hyde Park, NY 12538
www.ciachef.edu

❧

Throughout its history, The Culinary Institute of America has been committed to providing professional culinary education of the highest quality. Over the years, as our school has grown and our educational programs have evolved the values and ideas that influence our cooking have evolved as well.

The opening of our West Coast campus at Greystone in California's Napa Valley and the celebration of our 50th anniversary in 1996 provided a timely opportunity to take stock of our philosophy of food and cooking.

We hope that by stating these philosophical principles we will stimulate further discussion within and beyond the CIA community about the basic elements that constitute good food and fine cooking. While the CIA's New York and California campuses draw on their own specific and unique regional resources, both are committed to upholding our philosophy as well as facilitating full discussion and debate about these important issues. We will fully explore the topic of "The Sustainable Kitchen" at the first Joe Baum Forum of the Future to be held at the Institute's Hyde Park campus on September 24th and 25th.

- *Simplicity and Attention to Detail.* In cooking we strive for simplicity in concept and attention to detail in execution, especially in matters of flavor and taste.

- *Mastery of the Fundamentals.* Whether it's knife skills, braising or grilling techniques, the fine points of naturally leavened bread, the transformation of rice into risotto, or the tempering of chocolate, understanding and mastery of the basics is essential to good cooking and baking. These techniques of the professional kitchen are the result of knowledge accumulated and refined over generations. One of our chief responsibilities is to educate students in the fundamentals, thereby ensuring that this legacy continues to be strengthened and passed on to future generations.

- *Cooking and Baking Traditions of Many Cultures.* Cultural diversity is at the core of our educational programs and restaurants. Rather than ranking the world's cuisine—one above the other—we recognize that many cultures have achieved a measure of greatness in their culinary and baking traditions. These traditions, often based in the home, deserve to be more widely studied and enjoyed.

- *Innovation and Tradition.* We actively encourage culinary innovation based on respect for our cooking traditions that have evolved over generations. We ask that chefs and cooks endeavor to thoroughly understand the historical and cultural contexts of a dish before reworking it into something new. And we hope that some chefs will take up the charge of preservation and authenticity with the same passion that others bring to innovation.

- *Food Safety and Sanitation.* We respect the lives and health of our customers, co-workers, friends, and families. Therefore, Those of us who are involved with the preparation and serving of food have a continual obligation to ensure the acquisition of pure, uncontaminated food; the cleanliness of kitchen, bakery, and pastry shop work environments; and the observance of proper food-handling techniques.

- *Good Ingredients and Seasonal Flavors.* Good cooking begins with good ingredients. The fresh, seasonal flavors of our gardens, and the gardens and farms of our regions, inspire our cooking and shape our menus. Beyond enhancing flavor and texture, buying seasonal food lowers costs.

- *Taste Over Appearance.* We seek excellence of flavor and superior nutritional value in the produce we grow and buy, and are willing to accept odd shapes, sizes, and, if necessary, a few surface imperfections. Insistence on cosmetic perfection in fruits and vegetables leads plant breeding and variety selection away from taste, and requires excessive use of potentially harmful pesticides.

- *Sustainable Agriculture.* We seek out foods that have been grown or produced through environmentally sustainable methods. We use such methods to cultivate the gardens that supply our teaching facilities and restaurants. We support humane animal husbandry and wherever possible, purchase meat and poultry grown without hormones or antibiotic feed additives.

- *Links with Growers.* We are committed to maintaining and strengthening traditions of regional agriculture in this country. In our food purchasing, we emphasize direct relationships with smaller growers in the respective areas of our two campuses. We believe that supporting regional farmers' markets is part of our community responsibility. We applaud the efforts of large growers to respond to concerns about flavor and sustainability as they work to fulfill the needs and interests of consumers. We believe that chefs and all those who care about good food should understand agriculture and the challenges that both large and small farms face in bringing affordable high-quality food to the marketplace.

• *Processing of Foods.* We emphasize whole, minimally processed foods in our cooking in order to retain valuable nutrients and non-nutritive substances as well as enhance natural flavors in finished dishes. Recognizing the demand of contemporary consumers for convenience in foods, we encourage food manufacturing that builds on healthful ingredients and techniques of traditional home-based food processing.

• *Increased Emphasis on Plant Foods.* We support diets and cooking that focus on plant foods. In view of the high incidence of preventable, diet-linked chronic diseases in this country, we have an obligation to demonstrate that plant foods—fruits and vegetables, breads and grains, beans and other legumes, nuts and natural plant oils—can form the core of critically acclaimed meals and highly palatable, healthful diets. We support the scientific view that as long as long as calories are sufficient in a diet and variety is emphasized, largely plant-based diets provide all the necessary protein and essential nutrients we need for strong and healthy bodies while minimizing the risk for diet-related cancers, heart disease, and other chronic ailments. We single out increased consumption of fruits and vegetables as a priority, and as a special challenge to cooks and chefs.

- *Fish, Poultry, Dairy Products, Eggs Met in Smaller Amounts.* We recognize and appreciate the healthful traditions of the many cultures that use meat, poultry, fish, cheese, and other foods from animal sources to flavor diets based largely on plant foods. We also recognize that restaurants are places to celebrate special occasions, and on occasion, a healthful diet can include larger portions of food from animal sources.

- *Cooking with Plant Oils, Less Saturated Fat.* We use natural plant oils, emphasizing those high in monounsaturated fat, and minimizing the sue of saturated fat and hydrogenated fats in cooking, baking, and at the table. We use animal fats sparingly, whenever the flavor of butter, cream, lard, or other fat is especially appealing or critical to the success of a dish. We do not use margarine, artificial fats, or reduced-fat products where the flavor and integrity of the product has been compromised in the production process.

- *Total Fat, Calories and Health.* We note with interest the view of many scientists that diets low in saturated fat and largely plant-based may not necessarily need to be low in total fat in order to prevent heart disease, various cancers, and other chronic diseases. Given the role that fat plays in enhancing palatability, we believe that moderate levels of unsaturated fat may be important in persuading many people to adopt diets abundant in vegetables, grains, and legumes. We recognize that fat is a rich source of calories in the diet, and that too many calories in the diets of many Americans—from any source—is a leading public health concern. But we agree with scientists who believe that to achieve and maintain healthy weight, what is essential for most people is balancing total energy intake or calories with energy expenditure.

- *Exercise and Active Lifestyles.* A physically active lifestyle is a natural partner to a healthful diet. As professionals involved in feeding people in a culture with an overabundant food supply, we have an obligation to increase awareness of the life-enhancing benefits of exercise and other physical activity. We are heartened by the fact that active lifestyles lessen the need to restrict what we eat in order to lower chronic disease risk.

- *Wine and Healthful Diets.* We relish the proximity of both CIA campuses to wine regions for the unique educational opportunities they afford. Experimental and cross-cultural research confirms the healthful role that responsible wine consumption can play in the diets and lifestyles of many people.

- *Sharing Food, Drink, and the Pleasures of the Table.* We actively affirm the contribution that sharing food and drink can make toward nourishing friendships and building community. As part of our educational efforts, we highlight the ways in which foods, wines, and other beverages complement each other, further enhancing the pleasures of the table.

- *Affordability of Good Food.* While many special foods often cost more, excellence in cooking need not mean extra expense. Honest, pure food should be within everyone's grasp. We are committed to exploring new ways to translate affordable, fresh, seasonal healthful, multi-ethnic flavors into all types of food service and retail settings.

- *Mutual Respect and Appreciation.* Successful professional cooking is a team effort. As leaders in the foodservice industry and in culinary education, we treat our team members with respect and appreciation, and foster an environment where all can grow.

- *Diversity of Views and Lifelong Learning.* Continuing education and lifelong earning are fundamental to sustaining leadership. The ideas we have about food, drink, agriculture, and nutrition are the result of the information that is available to us. As research advances, beliefs and ideas evolve. Recognizing this, we fully support continuing research and ongoing discussion on the entire spectrum of food, culinary, health, agricultural, environmental, business, economic, and social issues.

Individual and Global Needs

Terri Brownlee

Nutrition Department
Duke Diet and Fitness Center, Duke Center for Living
804 West Trinity Avenue
Durham, North Carolina 27701-1826
http://dmi-www.mc.duke.edu/dfc/home.html

❧

The prevalence of obesity has become epidemic in the American population, afflicting more than one-half of the adult population as well as a growing number of children. This trend, which has been most dramatic in the past few decades, shows no signs of slowing down despite the $30 billion spent annually on weight loss programs and products by Americans. The true costs, however, for individuals carrying excessive weight are the increased risks for heart disease, diabetes, hypertension, various cancers, joint problems, gallstones and other diseases. It is estimated that obesity-related conditions contribute to 300,000 deaths yearly, ranking second only to smoking as a cause of preventable death.

The Duke Diet & Fitness Center program (DFC) was developed to address the needs of the overweight individual with an emphasis on both weight loss and overall health improvement. The DFC offers expertise in fitness, nutrition, behavior and medicine and provides the individual with all of the necessary skills to reach their goals and create a healthy, sustainable lifestyle.

Sustainability has been the missing ingredient of many of the weight-loss approaches used by Americans. Indeed, losing weight is a major challenge. However, maintaining weight loss while enjoying life has proved to be the greater obstacle. A familiar feeling to those who diet chronically is aptly described with the saying:

"Following this diet, will I actually live longer, or will it just seem like it?"

Sustainability can be viewed globally or as we approach it here, on an individual basis. It is an educational process; it includes becoming aware of the amount and types of food that the body needs to function properly; the awareness of emotional factors related to food consumption; awareness of the body's hunger and satiety signals; and awakening to the physical benefits of movement and activity.

Sustainable cuisine, defined here as having an enjoyable diet that has variety, balance and moderation, perhaps is the most challenging aspect for individuals seeking to control their weight today. Portion sizes have grown drastically in the last 20 years with more emphasis on value and the advent of the "super size" mentality. The average cola has increased from 8 ounces to 20–60 ounces; the average order of French fries has doubled; and a typical restaurant steak serving, which was once 8–12 ounces, is now 16–22 ounces. The National Restaurant Association estimates that Americans eat out an average of 4 meals per week, many of which are at all-you-can eat buffets.

This trend of "more is better" and the increase in affordability has led to the excessive intake of both animal products and highly processed foods. As a result, the consumption of whole grains, legumes, fruits, and vegetables has for many become a small percentage of total calories consumed despite the fact that our markets offer a greater variety than ever. Excessive calorie intake has become the norm and, with the decline in job-related physical activity, has proven to be a recipe for disaster.

Reversing this trend demands both an increase in knowledge and awareness, but lasting results require a total change in lifestyle. Noticing all aspects of food, the color, texture and aroma, and appreciating the freshness and ripeness are facets that enable one to embrace the philosophy of quality over quantity. Taking the time to enjoy a relaxed meal in a peaceful setting, in itself, is a great stride toward healthy nourishment. On a deeper level, having gratitude for the mother earth, the sun, the soil, the rain and those responsible for bringing the food to our plate creates a greater awareness and connection to the life-sustaining processes.

We encourage individuals to work toward grains, fruits and vegetables as a basis for their diets. Although many people cannot or will not sustain a totally vegetarian diet, we continue to work with individuals to view animal products as garnish. The individual who successfully shifts their diet to include more grains, fruits, vegetables, legumes, nuts and fewer animal products, not only greatly improves their own health, but greatly improves global health. Plant foods undeniably require fewer resources to produce and their production is healthier on our soil, water, and air. But greater benefits are gained when overall lifestyles are changed, and one becomes aware of the impact of all of their choices. Ultimately, global sustainability comes from the individual change that is, in itself, sustainable. We at the Duke Diet & Fitness Center are dedicated to helping people create and sustain lifestyle change.

—— ∞∞∞ ——

The Power
of Real Cheese

Jonathan White

Egg Farm Dairy
2 John Walsh Blvd.
Peekskill, NY 10566
www.creamery.com

For 8,000 years, there has been a triangle trade between humans, ruminants and lactic bacteria.

The humans protect and feed the livestock: sheep, cows, goats, camels, yaks, etc., while they graze on the grass and produce milk. This milk making is the result of another triangle, where the sun and soil produces grass, the cow eats the grass, and the manure fertilizes the soil.

Because the sun-grass cycle is seasonal, there is more milk in spring and less in winter. So, to balance the supply and demand, humanity developed a partnership with friendly bacteria, which ferment the surfeit spring milk into a preservable form: cheese. In subsistence agriculture, the spring milk stored as cheese was often times all that stood between the farm family and starvation.

Cheese is made by humans with the help of friendly bacteria. We "farm" the bacteria, feeding, nurturing and protecting them, allowing them to expand beyond their original domain, the teats of mammals. They in turn drink of milk's sweetness, cheating their nasty cousins, the spoiler organisms. They turn the sweet lactose into lactic acid, which causes the milk to curdle, and the curds to give up their water as whey. When it has shed its tears of whey, ephemeral milk becomes stable cheese, which is put in the cave or cellar, to await the pangs of winter.

There, in the cave, a hungry human, taking the last wheel of cheese, covered with mold, ripe almost to the point of rot, and, scraping away the oozing rind, in a triumph of the human spirit, tastes the fecundity of Spring on a frozen February morning.

In the 20th Century, this simple, balanced triangle devolved into a top-heavy system involving tanker trucks moving milk hundreds of miles to massive, capital intensive processing plants, producing rivers of wastewater and plastic-entombed lumps of orange stuff ironically still called "cheese."

But now we stand on the threshold of a rebirth, of the return of cheese making to the provinces, where cheeses reflect the uniqueness of their artisanal birth and the whey, and the value, stays on the farm. And since cheese has 10% of the mass of the milk that made it, we save 90% of the fossil fuel burned in transport.

We all carry within us the genetic memory of that cold February morning—it is indeed the reason that fermented foods hold such a deep spiritual appeal. Those of us who have seen the light have a responsibility to share the vision, to awaken the memory in others, so that demand for artisanal cheeses will reach a sustainable level and make them more affordable.

At the same time, we need to help lower the barriers that prevent fine artisanal products from reaching us. Small producers lack the capital required to age cheese properly, and the tractor-trailer retail food industry is simply not equipped to distribute and market artisanal products. The solution lies in establishment of regional aging consortia, which would buy young cheeses from farmers and sell ripe cheeses via the Web to citizens of the Global Village.

The last time we tore a page off of the millennial calendar, the world was undergoing a restructuring, as small kingdoms were once again being integrated into huge empires. Change can be good, and it can be bad, but it is always inevitable and irresistible. We can't stop the river of change from flowing, but we can steer it. And to the extent that we can direct those waters towards the floating of the human spirit, so we can measure our progress as a society.

Eat Sustainable, Eat Safe

Environmental Working Group

1718 Connecticut Avenue, NW, Suite 600
Washington, DC 20009
www.ewg.org

What can you do to reduce your intake of pesticides? Knowing which foods contain the largest amounts of pesticides is the first step.

Environmental Working Group obtained data from the US Food and Drug Administration on the amount of pesticides in 42 fruits and vegetables. We found that more than half of the total dietary risk from pesticides in these foods was concentrated in just 12 crops.

The 12 most contaminated foods:

1. Strawberries
2. Bell Peppers (Green and Red)
3. Spinach (tied for second)
4. Cherries
5. Peaches

6. Cantaloupe (Mexican)
7. Celery
8. Apples
9. Apricots
10. Green Beans
11. Grapes (Chilean)
12. Cucumbers

What does this mean for consumers? We recommend that you purchase produce with less pesticides on them. By avoiding the most contaminated produce, consumers will substantially reduce their dietary pesticide risks.

Thanks to the bounty of fruits and vegetables in most American supermarkets, people can radically minimize consumption of the 12 most contaminated fruits and vegetables with no nutritional risk. All of the vitamins, nutrients and carotenoids provided by the crops on the list of the 12 most contaminated are found in abundance in other fruits and vegetables available in just about any grocery store. In fact, few of the 12 most contaminated foods, with the notable exceptions of spinach, provide high levels of vitamins and carotenoids. A quick review of the list reveals plenty of equally nutritious, and safer, substitute foods.

Strawberries are a good source of vitamin C, but vitamin C is very common in fruits and vegetables. Nutritious substitutes with far lower pesticide residues are blueberries, raspberries, blackberries, kiwis and a host of other fruits rich in vitamin C.

Green bell peppers are a good source of vitamin C and red bell peppers add vitamin A and a moderate dose of carotenoids to a meal. Good alternatives include broccoli, romaine lettuce or carrots.

Spinach is rich in vitamins, iron, folate (folic acid) and carotenoids. Other greens such as kale, Swiss chard, mustard greens and collard greens are good nutritional substitutes, but have a roughly equivalent pesticide contamination profile. For raw spinach, romaine lettuce is far less contaminated alternative that is relatively high in carotenoids. For cooked spinach, broccoli or brussels sprouts are reasonable substitutes that are high in carotrnoids, vitamins A and C and folate. Cherries are a marginal source of vitamin C, but have little other nutritional value. Nutritional substitutes with far lower pesticide residues are blueberries, raspberries, blackberries, kiwis, oranges, watermelon and a host of other fruits rich in vitamin C.

Peaches provide relatively low amounts of vitamin A and C and negligible amounts of carotenoids. Nectarines, tangerines, cantaloupe and watermelon provide more vitamins A and C, and many other fruits such as oranges, grapefruits, papayas or kiwis provide high levels of one of these two vitamins.

Cantaloupe is a highly nutritious fruit packed with carotenoids and over 90 percent of the US Recommended Daily Allowance for vitamins A and C. To avoid cantaloupes with high pesticide residues, hold off on this fruit during January through April, when imports from Mexico are at their peak. The rest of the year, enjoy this marvelous melon.

Celery is a marginal source of carotenoids, but provides virtually no vitamins or minerals. Romaine lettuce and carrots are just two of the many safer salad substitutes.

Apples provide low amounts of vitamin C, but provide very little else in the way of measurable nutrients or carotenoids. Safer and more nutritious substitutes would include just about any fruit or vegetable not on the most contaminated list.

Apricots are nutritious fruit providing relatively high level carotenoids, vitamins A and C and potassium. An equally nutritious and safer substitute is cantaloupe from the US. A host of other fruits and vegetables provide vitamins A, C and other nutrients.

Green beans provide modest amounts of vitamins C, A and potassium, but little in the way of carotenoids. Safer and more nutritious alternatives include green peas, broccoli, zucchini, potatoes and many other vegetables.

Grapes are tasty, but provide few vitamins or carotenoids. The solution for grape lovers is simple: eat US grown grapes in season and avoid grapes from January through April, when grapes from Chile dominate the market.

Cucumbers have few vitamins or carotenoids. Substitutes for cucumbers include just about any vegetable not included on the most contaminated list.

Some foods are low in pesticides and pesticide risks and high in vitamins, minerals, and carotenoids. Sweet potatoes, broccoli, watermelon, and Brussels sprouts fit this bill, providing lots of vitamins, carotenoids and minerals, along with relatively few pesticides.

To complement the 12 most contaminated crops, we present the twelve cleanest crops. While no one should eat only these 12 foods, it is noteworthy that the fruits and vegetables with the lowest contamination scores also provide a broad array of nutritional health benefits.

The 12 cleanest crops are:

1. Avocados
2. Corn
3. Onions
4. Sweet Potatoes
5. Cauliflower
6. Brussels sprouts
7. Grapes
8. Bananas
9. Plums
10. Green Onions
11. Watermelon
12. Broccoli

———∞∞∞———

Fair Trade for a Fair Cuisine

Rodney North

Equal Exchange, Inc.
251 Revere Street
Canton, MA USA 02021
www.equalexchange.com

Whether your work is with sustainable agriculture, quality foods, economic development, social justice or supporting family farms, much of what is promising and what is wrong with today's food production can be found in the specialty and organic coffee sector.

Specialty coffee (the highest quality grade) has enjoyed tremendous growth in North America over the last 20 years and its annual retail sales in the US now exceed $2 billion dollars, even while overall coffee sales are flat or declining. In its wake certified organic coffee has since emerged as a second wave, is growing at an even faster rate, and already amounts to approximately $100 million in annual sales. Over 60 US coffee roasters now offer at least some organic coffees. This trend—flat total consumption married to a switch to higher quality and followed by an embrace of organic products—mirrors encouraging movements in other foods such as produce and breads.

Unfortunately, the coffee industry also offers insights into important weaknesses in our overall food production systems, in particular:

- Exploitative and ultimately unsustainable human relationships still abound in the agriculture sector;

- There is a critical shortage of investment capital in the "weak links" of (a) sustainable agriculture in developing countries, and (b) small farmer export financing.

In the 14 years that our cooperative, Equal Exchange, has been importing and marketing our line of specialty grade, organic coffees we have learned that to truly support sustainable agriculture one must begin from a comprehensive awareness of the entire food production chain, from those that finance the farmer to the supermarket shopper. And as one assembles that larger picture, one can begin to shore up, and reform the weakest sectors.

In our own industry we have seen that coffee production is disturbingly reliant on millions of poor, isolated, small scale farmers, and equally poor and marginalized plantation labor (sometimes the same small farmers). While the laborers' plight bears a resemblance to that of sweatshop workers, the small farmers' economic trap is less familiar to the North American public. There are millions of small coffee farmers and they provide as much as half of the world's total production, but individually they are vulnerable producers.

A typical coffee growing family:

• Has only a small plot, 5 acres or less;

• Is dependent upon one local buyer;

• Has no access to coffee market information;

• Has no access to reasonable financing, and some-times cannot escape becoming trapped in debt to the local buyer;

• Lacks information and training about adopting sustainable agricultural methods.

And, as an example of the larger system's dependence upon the vulnerability of these small producers, farmers often encounter violent resistance when they try to form cooperatives amongst themselves as alternatives to the local buyers, processors and exporters. Many organizers and co-op leaders have been assassinated, even long after the cooperatives have been established. No system built with, and dependent upon, force can be accepted, let alone called "sustainable."

Equal Exchange, and our European counterparts (including Café Direct, Twin Trading, and the Fair

Trade Labeling Organizations, FLO), in coordination with organizations representing small coffee farmers, have begun to address these problems by adopting what are called the standards of fair trade. Fair trade means that as importers:

- We buy our coffee directly from democratically run cooperatives of small scale farmers, thereby allowing farmers to capture the entire export price, instead of just a small fraction.

- We guarantee to pay at least $1.26 F.O.B. per pound of green coffee, or the world market price, whichever is higher. The "floor" price insures that the farmers' costs of production are covered, protecting them from the market's unpredictable and sometimes persistent low prices. (Note: today the world price is only $1.04 per pound, and from Sept. '89 to May '94 the price averaged about only 80 cents per pound, once reaching as low as 50 cents.)

- We offer affordable advance credit (more on this below).

- We encourage sustainable agriculture. We pay a 15 cent per pound premium on certified organic coffee and are always trying to increase our organic coffee imports. For example, this year 70% of our coffee imports are certified organic and shade grown. When necessary we will also assist a group trying to gain first time organic certification.

Now that these farmers have direct access to the export market and higher prices they have more options and can choose to focus on quality as a logical development strategy. Farmers can make the most of their small plots, and the lower yields of shaded, organic production by maximizing quality, and therefore income. So, whereas before there was little incentive to improve quality, the farmers are now paid a premium to grow the speciality grade Equal Exchange coffee that is, for example, served in some of New York City's best hotels, such as the Royalton and the SoHo Grand.

While Equal Exchange has had the "fair trade" coffee market to ourselves, we are also encouraging other coffee importers and roasters to join us and adopt fair trade standards. To make that switch easier, and to discourage fair trade opportunists, a non-profit third party certifier, TransFair USA, has been created along the lines of other consumer seal programs. TransFair authenticates for the consumer that a certain line of coffee has been imported on fair trade terms and grants the coffee roaster a "fairly traded" seal to put on the coffee package or bulk coffee bin. Our own experience suggests that with sufficient consumer education, and supportive shareholders, a company can absorb the higher costs of goods entailed under fair trade and still generate an acceptable profit.

Just as sustainable cuisine relies on sustainable agriculture, sustainable agriculture requires sustainable investment. While our domestic stock market seems awash with capital, only a very small portion of those resources are being channeled to those companies and organizations working along the chain of sustainable agriculture. And much of that money is going to a few large natural food retailers and food manufacturers. This might be in part because of a presumption about the "pulling" power of the market —if people want something, such as organic foods, someone else is going to provide it. However, few investors are dedicated to promoting sustainable cuisine, and those that are are unlikely to recognize the need to back small organic farmers in the developing world. This is happening at the same time that an increasing amount of our food needs are met by imports from developing countries, and multinational companies are gaining increased access to operate and buy land in these same countries. A possible result is that the uncapitalized, poor, small organic farmers might be squeezed out of the natural food markets altogether by large, well-capitalized, agro-industry.

The small farmer cooperatives were quick to educate us, the fair trade importers, about their needs for sufficient financing if they were to compete with other local coffee exporters. For example, even if the cooperatives received a high price, and could offer farmers a better price, they could do so only once their coffee was exported. In contrast, a local buyer typically possessed working capital and could pay a farmer for their coffee much sooner, albeit not as much. To meet this problem fair traders now offer affordable pre-shipment financing. With those funds co-ops can now pay their members earlier, and thereby meet the threat posed by other buyers. But coffee is expensive and fair traders, and their supporting organizations (such as Shared Interest, Ltd., a "solidarity" lending institute in the UK) need to be capitalized themselves if they are to extend financing to the farmer cooperatives. In addition to fair traders, there are other organizations (CEPAD in Nicaragua, TechnoServe in the US, EDSC in the Netherlands, Christian Aid in the UK, among others) that have begun to work out how to meet the long-term investment needs of these small farmer cooperatives.

We have only worked out the process for funding these small farmers. Actual investment backing still needs to be found before we can strengthen this remaining weak link in the sustainable agriculture chain.

—◦∞◦—

A Sustainable Diet for the New Millennium

Jim Rosen, Chairman of the Board

Fantastic Foods
1250 North McDowell Street
Petaluma, CA 94951
www.fantasticfoods.com

❧

The advent of the millennium presents an ideal opportunity to make lifestyle changes that will enhance our health and well being, and preserve and sustain our fragile planet.

Sustainable cuisine means more than simply feeding a hunger. It takes into account what we put into our mouths, where it comes from, how it's produced, what it does to our bodies and how it affects the Earth. The hallmarks of a diet based on sustainable cuisine define the secrets of health, enable us to live on the Earth sustainably, help us think compassionately about all living creatures, and encourage us to consider and honor our connection to all living beings.

Even with high-tech farming methods now employed worldwide, chronic hunger still affects upwards of 1.3 billion people. Forty to 60 million people will starve to death on the planet this year. If we're having a difficult time feeding the 6 billion people currently populating the Earth, how are we going to fill the stomachs of the 9 billion people expected to inhabit our planet by 2032? It's time we faced this crisis. There is an answer and sustainable cuisine can help.

By far, the way to begin is to cut back on meat consumption. Frances Moore Lappe in her book, *Diet for a Small Planet*, discovered the staggering amounts of grain necessary to feed the livestock that are the center of a meat-based diet. For example, it takes 16 pounds of grain to produce a pound of feed-lot beef. It takes only one pound of grain to produce a pound of bread.

Today, livestock consume 10 times more grain than Americans eat directly. Most of us assume that farm exports go to feed the hungry around the world when, in reality, two-thirds of all agricultural exports go to feed livestock. Only a very small minority of hungry people in Third World countries can afford beef and, even with a huge jump in grain exports, malnutrition is still the principal cause of infant and child mortality in developing nations.

If Americans were to reduce their meat consumption by only 10 percent, enough grain would be saved to feed 60 million people. It is not necessary to eat meat to get enough protein. A variety of plant foods could meet our dietary needs, and we could safely choose not to eat animal products and remain healthy.

A meat-centered diet increases the chances of ingesting harmful pesticides. Each year, an estimated 911 million pounds of synthetic pesticides are applied to conventional agricultural crops throughout the United States. When livestock eat treated grain and grass, pesticide residues concentrate in their tissues. A Food and Drug Administration (FDA) study found the most pesticides (22 percent) in meat, fish and poultry compared to fruits and vegetables.

In addition, the massive quantities of waste produced by livestock and poultry threaten rivers, lakes and other waterways. In the United States, where waste generated by livestock is 130 times that produced by humans, livestock wastes are implicated in waterway pollution, toxic algae and fishkills, according to the Worldwatch Institute.

We encourage everyone to make a commitment to the Earth, its creatures and your own health by adopting a more sustainable diet.

Here's how you can do it:

- Eliminate or reduce consumption of all animal proteins including meat, poultry, milk, eggs and cheese. Replace them not with their low-fat versions but with a wide variety of vegetables, grains and fruits.

- Increase fiber-containing foods such as whole grains, vegetables and fruits. In other words, eat lower on the food chain as often as possible.

- Eat plant-based foods taken from different parts of the plants including the roots, stems, leaves and flowers (broccoli florets), seeds and fruits. This will ensure that you take in a wide variety of health-giving vitamins, minerals, antioxidants and other phytochemicals.

- Read labels. Educate yourself about additives such as gelatin and rennet which are animal derived.

- Speak up. Ask about ingredients at the market or in restaurants. Tell retailers what you like and don't like about the products they're selling.

- Make a difference one meal at a time. Challenge yourself and your family to eat at least one more vegetarian meal a week. Do it for your health and the health of the planet as we approach the millennium.

Sustainable Cuisine in the Fridge

Jason Englander

FreshTech™
411 West Putnam Avenue, Suite 303
Greenwich, CT 06830

❧

FreshTech is a company formed for the purpose of assisting food purveyors, food growers, food transporters, food warehousemen and your local market to extend the shelf life of foods and reduce harmful gases and odors in the refrigerated environment.

Our mission is to keep food fresher longer from grower to transporter to warehouse to market to home and ultimately to the dinner table.

We keep food fresher longer by applying principles of moisture and ethylene gas control in a user-friendly format. FreshTech is aware of the food spoilage problem both commercially and at home and, therefore, manufactures both commercial and residential products.

FreshTech promotes sustainable cuisine by allowing more people to enjoy more food by reducing waste, thereby amplifying the supply of food by extending the shelf life of food products.

A side benefit of the use of the FreshTech product commercially, allows refrigerator equipment to operate more efficiently. We have empirically shown that by reducing condensation and frost buildup on refriger-ation coils, typical refrigeration equipment will use up to 50% less energy to cool foods with our prod-uct. Reducing condensation and frost buildup also increases the efficiency and reduces the necessary maintenance on the refrigeration units, thereby reducing the amount of time the cooling unit has to run to maintain a stated temperature. Keeping the insulation dry increases the refrigerated container's ability to retain cold air. Scientific tests have indi-cated that when the insulation becomes moist from humidity, it becomes a conductor of heat, rather than an insulator. It is axiomatic that a unit that runs less and operates more efficiently will last longer.

We recognize that no one contribution can claim to be the primary source of sustainable cuisine. We would like to believe that FreshTech is making its contribution to sustaining the freshness of foods, the ambience of foods, increasing the abundance of available fresh produce, vegetables and meats thereby making America's, indeed the world's, table more appetizing, healthful and satisfying.

Food Choices and Our Environment

Sarah Newport
Friends of the Earth

Friends of the Earth
1025 Vermont Avenue NW, 3rd Floor
Washington, DC, 20005
www.foe.org

~&

Few of us today have any real connection with the people or farms that sustain us. Most of the food we eat is grown and transported from thousands of miles away, making it difficult to know how it was produced. As a result, we may eat fruits and vegetables that have been sprayed with dangerous chemicals, and inadvertently support farming practices that waste energy and pollute our air and water.

With its emphasis on uniformity and mass production, "industrialized" agriculture has reduced food prices for the average American consumer, but it has taken its toll on the environment, our health and community structure.

"Between 1964 and 1994, pesticide use in the United States doubled from 500 million to over 1 billion pounds per year," according to John Wargo, Environment Sciences Professor at Yale University.

Pesticides and fertilizer run off fields with rainfall, polluting the nation's lakes, streams, rivers and estuaries and threatening drinking water supplies. In fact, agriculture is the greatest source of pollution in the United States, according to recent studies.

Pesticides are poisons intended to kill bacteria, weeds, insects and fungus, but they can also harm animals and humans. The National Academy of Sciences has classified more than 80% of the most commonly used pesticides as carcinogenic. Pesticides can also harm immunological and reproductive systems by mimicking human hormones.

How can you be sure your food is free of harmful pesticides residues? Food labels provide "nutrition facts" on fat, calories and vitamins, but disclose nothing about a food's pesticide content. Take the apple you had with lunch, for instance. It may have been grown on a large-scale orchard that used several pesticides and fertilizers to ensure strong crop yields. An astonishing 61% of apples tested recently by the Food and Drug Administration (FDA) were contaminated with pesticides. Children are most at risk from pesticide contaminated foods, because they often consume more per body weight of certain foods that contain pesticide residues, such as fruits.

Ironically, despite the enormous increase in pesticide use since 1945, the percentage of crops destroyed by pests has hardly changed. Insects that have been sprayed with pesticides are evolving resistant forms, requiring farms to apply even greater quantities of these chemicals.

As corporations dominate more and more aspects of food production, they are preventing farmers from controlling even the most basic element of agriculture, the seed. Historically, seeds were a renewable resource. Farmers could save the seeds produced from one year's harvest to plant the next. Today, many seeds are hybrid varieties produced by crossbreeding two or more species. These hybrids yield food but the crops produce sterile seeds, forcing farmers to buy new seeds each year. The technology involved in developing these seeds enables corporations to patent them and actually bars farmers from saving seeds for reuse. For example, Monsanto, which recently merged with American Home Products, has claimed the patent for all the future genetically engineered products of the entire species of cotton and soybeans.

Since farmers must now pay corporations for the right to plant seeds, many small farmers are going out of business. And native people in developing countries, who have cultivated and improved crops for thousands of years, are forced to pay corporations for their seeds. As a result, the local, less profitable crop species—critical to a sustainable agricultural system—are no longer grown.

A growing number of farms are rejecting chemical-intensive, industrialized agriculture and instead raising food produced without pesticides, fertilizers, hormones and animal cruelty. "Sustainable agriculture" conserves the soil for future generations, treats livestock humanely and uses non-toxic water and energy-efficient farming techniques.

Sustainable agriculture requires farmers to take responsibility for their impact on consumer health. But while the success of sustainable farming largely depends on visionary farmers bucking the corporate trend, consumers must take some share of the responsibility. Sustainable cuisine is a positive step in the right direction. Vice President Al Gore had noted that "more and more, consumer power will work against pesticide pollution, even when government does not." All of us can help by purchasing locally grown organic produce; shopping at food co-ops or farmers' markets; and growing our own fruits and vegetables or supporting a community garden.

Growing Sustainably, the DC Example

Matthew Hora

From the Ground Up
645 Taylor Street, NE
Washington DC 20017

❧

From the Ground Up is a community farm project that is sponsored by the Capital Area Food Bank (CAFB) and the Chesapeake Bay Foundation (CBF). This uncommon marriage between the anti-hunger and environmental movements is a particularly revealing indication that active and collaborative solutions are required to address the inequities and abuses within our food production and distribution systems.

With a 285-acre farm and staff support provided by CBF, the campaign to reduce nitrogen and phosphorus accumulation in the region's waterways benefits from a farm that uses no agricultural chemicals or farming practices that lead to erosion and nutrient imbalances. The CAFB provides the staff and funding for the farm, and in return there are increased outlets for fresh produce in underserved communities, a 30-mile driving distance from field to table. The program also serves as an example of a non-emergency feeding program that is less reliant upon traditional grant monies.

From the Ground Up was founded in 1992 in response to the lack of access to fresh produce in lower income neighborhoods throughout Washington, DC. Since 80% of food spending occurs at supermarkets, the flight of these outlets from the inner cities of America to the suburbs has left a vacuum in which smaller groceries try to meet the huge demand. Unfortunately, in Washington, DC there is a great disparity between outlets for fresh produce in different sections of the city, with the poorer areas often having no market within walking distance. This situation is further exacerbated by lower car ownership in these neighborhoods, an increased reliance on public transportation to simply buy groceries for a meal, and, of course, lower incomes. The founders of From the Ground Up decided to address this problem not by creating another emergency feeding program for the hungry, but by engaging a local farm to grow vegetables specifically for these populations, for many years to come.

The mission of the program: To develop a community that links urban and rural life through shared work, celebration, education and food. To provide access to fresh seasonal produce that are grown in a way that protects and enriches the land and its people.

The majority of our efforts are devoted to developing Community Supported Agriculture (CSA), which served more than 275 individuals in the metro DC area in 1998. In an era where the family milkman and green grocer are but fond memories, From the Ground Up aims to become a familiar face in the weekly eating habits of its customers. Besides receiving fresh produce, the community is invited to visit the Clagett Farm for weekend outings, seasonal festivals, and educational programs.

At the beginning of the season, customers purchase a "share" of the harvest, and in return the farmer provides a weekly bag of produce for the entire growing season. In some cases shareholders are involved in the decision-making process of the farming operation, selecting crops and rotations, deciding upon the share prices, and planning farm social events. From the Ground Up delivers the bulk of the shares throughout the DC area at eight drop-off sites where a staff member distributes the produce.

Despite an extended drought, the Clagett Farm soils produced over 85,000 pounds of vegetables in 1998. Last year From the Ground Up allocated 75 shares for people in demonstrable need of an inexpensive food supply, and reduced the price of their shares by half. Many of these shares were sold to food pantries, churches, and other organizations that were not accustomed to serving fresh vegetables to their clientele. The continued success of the CSA program is allowing From the Ground Up to steadily decrease its dependence upon outside funding, which has been a primary goal since its inception.

We all deserve the highest quality food and that's one reason we use environmentally sensitive growing techniques. We use organic pesticides only in emergencies, and use no herbicides, fungicides, or chemical fertilizers of any kind. Through crop rotations and an extensive cover cropping system, we aim to leave Clagett Farm in better condition than we found it, and to lessen the impact that agriculture has on the health of the Chesapeake Bay.

Our prices are based solely on the costs of production and distribution, which are kept to a minimum since we deal directly with the customers. Taste not transportation!

Since 1992 From the Ground Up has distributed more than 250,000 pounds of produce through the CSA. The CSA shareholders and other members of our wider community help to support local agriculture, promote our local economy, and help to feed those in need.

This season From the Ground Up will be operating a new farmers' market in the Anacostia neighborhood of Southeast Washington, DC. This market is intended to address the dual need for new and viable marketing opportunities for local farmers and to provide access to fresh and affordable produce in an underserved neighborhood. An added incentive to create a market in Anacostia was to tap into a tradition that the area's African-American population observes on a weekly basis, the Sunday family gathering and subsequent large meal.

The vision of From the Ground Up for the coming years is based around a regional food system that can support at least 25% of the produce needs of the area during the growing season. The inclusion of fresh and affordable produce at retail outlets in under-served neighborhoods and the return of large super-markets to the inner city need to occur so that all DC residents have equal access to fresh vegetables. The establishment of several CSA's will supply thousands of residents with their produce needs and support new farmers and farmers' markets.

To reduce the reliance on imported foods throughout the entire season, the eating habits of the American population need to change so that cheap and exotic foods aren't expected year round. And perhaps most importantly, to invest in the long term health of our food system, bring the children out to the farm to enjoy a day running around the wide open spaces of the farm, breathing fresh air and basking in the outdoors in a way that children have for centuries.

―――∽∞∞∽―――

Sustainable Cuisine, Part of Sustainable Living

Norma and Ingrid Homberg

gepa 3
P.O. Box 439
New York, NY 10276-0439
www.gepa3.com

❧

Sustainable cuisine is an important part of sustainable living. To consume products that represent caring for the earth, for the people growing and producing food products, and for the local economy from which the product comes is a good step toward helping yourself and your environment come closer to the goal of sustainability.

It is important to understand what makes a product "sustainable." For our company, sustainability is a combination of the social, ecological and economical factors.

Our company focuses on the issue of fair trade, which means we pay a higher "fair" price for our product so that farmers can reinvest the profits into their community and raise their standards of living. All our company's teas are packaged in hand-made recycled cotton cartons or hand-woven reed baskets. Not only does this create additional income for the local economies but it prevents polluting the environment with wasteful packaging.

We also focus on certified organic growth of all our products. Our teas are certified and inspected by Naturland, Demeter Institute for Market Ecology and IFOAM (International Federation of Organic Agricultural Movements). We have been growing our teas organically for 14 years now because we believe sustainability is more than organic agriculture—it means we don't tolerate exploiting the earth or its people.

We believe "sustainable products" such as our teas are grown with a philosophy and care that is reflected in their high quality. Our "mother ship," gepa Fairhandelshaus, based in Germany, has been working with Third World countries since 1975 to promote fair trade and sustainable agriculture. We joined gepa in 1996 to bring the company's wonderful products to the United States and Canada.

The gepa 3 mission reads "The promotion of social responsibility and sustainable ecological development." While it is frustrating that sustainability is in constant battle with greed it is more than a dream when each of us involved is making a difference. We need to make everyone aware that we cannot abuse planet earth and that we all need to take on responsibility for our planet. Supporting sustainable business as an individual can be as simple as changing your shopping habits. Organic products are becoming more accessible every day. And the best part is you are helping yourself at the same time.

What happens if we ignore sustainability? The consequences of environmental pollution are dramatic. In the field of agriculture, if we continue to use pesticides and herbicides it will lead to an exhaustion of our soil and our plants will become more susceptible to illnesses. Also, we cannot be sure what effects these pesticides and herbicides are having on our health. All the additives found in non-organic products may be the cause of certain cancers, asthma and skin disorders. We believe that no one should take that chance. In the end if it tastes better, and is better for your health and the environment, why not eat sustainable cuisine?

⸺⸺

An Industry with an Appetite for Fiber

Jeff Lindenthal

Green Field Paper Company
1330 G Street
San Diego, CA 92101
www.greenfieldpaper.com

I would like to apply the idea of "sustainable cuisine" to an industry that is consuming its raw material at a rate faster than can be sustained. I am referring to the paper industry and the consumption of cellulose fiber from which paper is made. Pulp derived from trees serves as the paper industry's main course and growing demand for fiber will exhaust supply.

At Green Field Paper Company, we manufacture paper from an alternative diet of fiber derived from hemp, organically grown cotton, waste paper and agricultural residues. The nature of our fiber-based manufacturing diet is best summarized by the notion of "waste = food," an equation coined by Paul Hawken in his seminal book *The Ecology of Commerce*.

This boiled-down equation has more relevance now for industry in general, and the paper industry in particular, than ever before. Paper consumption on a per capita basis in the US, already the highest of any country in the world, is steadily increasing. There is agreement within the paper industry that a "fiber shortage" is looming on the horizon. Just when the fiber shortage will occur is subject to debate but the fact is we are consuming paper at a pace that is not sustainable.

If we are harvesting trees to yield fiber for paper faster than we can replenish forest resources, where can the paper industry find alternative feedstocks? Let's return to the waste equals food equation. Waste paper certainly offers one viable feedstock. We need to capture and recycle more waste paper and increase the post consumer content of most recycled papers. Another plentiful fiber source is the byproduct of agriculture and our food growing systems. There are millions of tons of wheat straw, corn and cotton waste generated in the US each year. These waste materials are rich in fiber and have the potential to shake the paper industry's voracious appetite.

The best example I have observed of sustainable production in practice occurs in nature. The ecosystem at work in a forest is a fine example. Here, the deciduous leaves that fall to the forest floor degrade over time to create a rich layer of humus which nourishes the surrounding trees and plants—waste becomes food and nothing is wasted! Production systems such as organic farming that grow out of this simple model embrace sustainability and maximize efficiency.

The challenge we face in business is to apply this same principle to the methods we choose to produce goods and services. In our approach to paper making we opportunistically search for raw materials much like a chef surveying the refrigerator for leftover ingredients to transform into the next meal. In our cookbook of paper recipes we have borrowed a page from nature and allowed history to guide us.

For thousands of years worldwide, and more than three centuries in the US, paper has been made from non-wood fibers derived from textile waste and agricultural residues. To design our line of environmentally responsible paper we have returned to the roots of the American paper industry. By working in partnership with clothing manufacturers, coffee roasters and garlic farmers (among others) to recycle their production byproducts we are reinventing an age-old tradition of papermaking with the most environmentally friendly fibers of today.

In this mode of production, waste fiber becomes paper... a cycle which can and, with your participation, will be completed again and again. The paper samples tipped into this book represent the progress that has been made and elegantly demonstrate that the paper industry can supplement its diet of trees with feedstocks derived from non-wood fibers.

I Do Not Like Green Eggs and Ham!

Robert F. Kennedy, Jr

The word "sustainable" expresses the obligation that each generation has to the next to preserve the value of the natural world. It does not mean we can't use nature. Mankind, a predatory animal, is part of nature and in my view, the worst outcome of environmental advocacy is if it results in separating human beings from nature. God wants us to use the bounties of the Earth to enrich ourselves, to raise living standards, to build dignified vital communities, to savor life through all our senses and to serve others, we just can't use it up! We can live off the interest, we just can't go into the capital. This broad definition generally leaves me with a full plate. My own nature is to not be too careful about what I eat.

I avoid endangered species; monkey brains, shark

fins, whale sushi, sea turtle, and Atlantic swordfish, which, but for its endangered status, is my favorite food. Otherwise, I'll try almost anything on the menu or off the road. I've eaten all kinds of insects and nematodes, caterpillars, snakes, frogs, alligators, terrapins, sea urchins, octopus, birds eggs, a mouse (by mistake), wild game including armadillo, wildebeest, warthog, coons and capybara, and some domestic animals including horse, dog and guinea pig. I have eaten road kill and I'm fond of viscera; tripe, tongue, brain and offal and sweet meats and pate, kidney pie, sheep's eyes and even airline food. Ironically, bad example has been the professor of good ethics; my son is a vegetarian and can hardly bear to sit with me at meals.

Arguably, the most sustainable food is the hot dog since that's where they put all the stuff that would otherwise go to waste. It's like the Indians and the buffalo, they used everything. Buffalo hot dogs might be the best bet. Among all ungulents, buffalo use the prairies without destroying them. But most hot dogs are neither dogs nor buffalo but hogs and, nowadays, that means industrial pork which, next to an endangered species, is the worst food on earth.

North Carolina's hogs now outnumber its citizens and produce more fecal waste than all the people in California, New York and Washington combined. Some industrial pork farms produce more sewage than America's largest cities. But while human waste

must be treated, hog waste, similarly fetid and viru-
lent, is simply dumped into the environment.
Stadium sized warehouses shoehorn 100,000 sows
into claustrophobic cages that hold them in one position for a lifetime over metal grate floors. Below, alu-
minum culverts collect and channel their putrefying
waste into ten acre open air pits three stories deep
from which miasmal vapors choke surrounding communities and tens of millions of gallons of hog feces
ooze annually into North Carolina's rivers. Such
practices have created a science fiction nightmare
right out of Revelations. In North Carolina, the fes-
tering effluent that escapes from industrial swine
pens has given birth to *pfiesteria piscicida*, a toxic
microbe that thrives in the fecal marinade of North
Carolina rivers. This tiny predator, which can morph
into 24 forms depending on its prey species, inflicts
pustulating lesions on fish whose flesh it dissolves
with excreted toxins then sucks through a mouth
tube. The "cell from hell" has killed so many fish, —
a billion in one instance—that North Carolina must
use bulldozers to bury them beneath the rancid
shores of the Neuse River and Pamlico Sound.
Pfiesteria causes brain damage and respiratory illness
in humans who touch infected fish or water. Two
years ago, *Pfiesteria* sickened 36 fishermen and swim-
mers and 4 bridge workers who never even got damp.

Industrial farming is also for the birds. Some corporate
farms crowd a million beakless chickens in cramped
dark cages soaking up antibodies and laying their

guts out for modern mengales like Frank Perdue for the duration of their miserable lives. It's hard to believe that people who run those animal concentration camps will even enjoy happiness or dignity in their own lives.

And the chickens are coming home to roost. Industrial farming isn't just bad for chickens and hogs, it destroys family farms, aquifers, soils, and pollutes the air and water. Billionaire chicken barons Don Tyson and Frank Perdue, like billionaire North Carolina hog tycoon Wendell Murphy, have used their market power to drive a million family farmers out of business including virtually every independent egg and broiler farmer in America. Each corporate farm puts 10 family farmers out of business. The same process of vertical integration has bankrupted 5 out of 6 of America's hog farmers over the past 15 years and pushed the final nail in the coffin of Thomas Jefferson's vision of a democracy rooted in family owned freeholds. Industrial meat moguls site their stinking farms in the poorest communities and pay slave wages to their miniscule work force for performing one of the most dangerous and unhealthy jobs in America.

Massive political contributions by this tiny handful of billionaire AG-barons allow them to evade laws that prohibit other Americans from polluting our waterways. Industrial agriculture now accounts for over half of America's water pollution. Last year, *pfiesteria* outbreaks connected with wastes from industrial chicken factories forced the closure of two major tributaries of the Chesapeake and threatened Maryland's vital shellfish industry. Tyson Foods has polluted half of all streams in Northwest Arkansas with so much fecal bacteria that swimming is prohibited. Drugs and hormones needed to keep confined animals alive and growing are mainly excreted with the wastes and now saturate local waterways.

Moreover, industrial meat is unsavory. Factory raised meat and pork are soft and bland. The chicken doesn't taste good. American chicken is spongy. It's been around long enough that people have forgotten how chicken is supposed to taste and most young people erroneously think you are supposed to be able to cut chicken with a fork. The texture gives thoughts of hormones and chemicals.

Since you can't often tell the difference between meat and fowl from factory and family farms in the grocery store, it's not always easy to avoid industrial eggs and ham.

Chefs should look for free range chickens from suppliers they trust and seek out local markets and producers who buy from sustainable family farms. Those who look will find networks of sustainable family farms and farmers who raise their animals to range free on grass pastures and natural feeds without steroids, sub-therapeutic antibiotics or other artificial growth promotants and who treat their animals with dignity and respect.

These farmers bring tasty premium quality meat to customers while practicing the highest standards of husbandry and environmental stewardship.

One such production is California based Niman Ranch, which markets the highest quality Iowa and California pork and beef, antibiotic free and hormone free and ships to retailers and restaurateurs anywhere in the nation. Livestock are humanely treated, fed the purest natural feeds (with no animal by-products or waste), never given growth hormones or sub-thera-peutic antibiotics, and raised on lands that is cared for as a sustainable resource. Many restaurants list Niman Ranch on their menu.

Sustainable meats taste the best. This is another case where doing right means eating well.

A Dinner
We Can Pay For

Gavril Vissarion Lourie, Food Writer

533 Canal Street, 6th floor
New York, NY 10013
vissarion@hotmail.com

❧

Sustainable cuisine is a new phrase coined for an old concept—this planet has sustained not only ourselves but animals, reptiles, insects and fauna that number well beyond the trillions for millennia. Not only has this tiny blue eco-sphere sustained life, but also it has generated such an abundance of organisms that we are just becoming acquainted with some of them. How is it possible that such a rich and renewable source of life could ever become threatened by the human race? As powerful as we are, we only constitute a tiny fraction of the inhabitants of this planet. The impending problem lies in the perversity of our "diet."

Humans, because of their very nature, overcomplicate and ritualize even the most basic of nature's functions. The relationship between people and the sustenance they consume runs the gamut from the ritualistic, to the automatic, to the obsessive—but is almost never conscious. Ritual and religion have long had there influence on the way people eat, Muslim and kosher law have long forbade the eating of pork, which at one time was a healthy idea, due in part to the diseases carried by pigs. But now in a more hygienic society where pig diseases are not a problem, religious laws that favor cows as the main livestock are out of touch with the needs of an increasingly taxed planet. The pig is probably one of the most sustainable animals on the planet, practically a recycling center on four hooves.

People are not conscious of how their diet affects themselves let alone the earth. And the experts are not helping. Every six months the nutritionists turn their own rhetoric on its ear—protein is the new fiber! Those few of us with some nutritional knowledge seem to take leave of their senses as soon as a menu is placed in their hands. The task of raising the human consciousness to consider the planet as a whole every time people raise a fork to their mouth is considerable, to say the least.

When I think of saving the world through sustainable cuisine, certain paradoxes immediately come to mind—the image of hundreds of Vietnamese pedaling bicycles connected to generators to produce electricity and the Manhattan windows filled with New Yorkers pedaling those exercycles. Couldn't we connect generators to all those NYSC gym bikes and ship off the excess juice to Vietnam? Think of all the spring rolls and rice congee that would be saved by not having to feed the peddlers of Vietnam! And if that seems somewhat impractical, maybe those New Yorkers could cut a mere seventy thousand pastrami sandwiches a day (only one one-hundredth of a sandwich per person) out of their diet and could reduce a huge amount of that pedaling that gets them nowhere! It doesn't even keep the lights on. We could ship a giant barge with 2.1 million pastrami sandwiches a month to Vietnam, and I am damn sure they would be more appreciative than Virginia.

All kidding aside, when I am asked about sustainable cuisine I find myself referring to examples of China and India, densely populated nations which have sustained themselves for thousands of years on rice-based cuisines. One of the most important concepts in Eastern cuisine is adaptability, using whatever the earth gives you. The Chinese eat a variety of seafood that is truly staggering in contrast to the United States where we make pitiful use of our marine resources, and most people find squid "exotic."

We need to combine the lessons of the past and our knowledge of the eco-system to prepare a dinner we can pay for.

Food With a Face, a Place, a Taste

Russell Libby, Executive Director

Maine Organic Farmers and Gardeners Association
283 Water Street, 4th Floor
Augusta, Maine 04338
www.mofga.org

❧

A first step towards a sustainable cuisine is to acknowledge we don't have one now. Now the source of our food is everywhere and nowhere— everywhere because affluent consumers can buy food from anywhere in the world, and nowhere because there is no personal connection that traces the food back to a particular farmer's field.

The most memorable meals of my life are intimately connected to family and friends, to foods that came from our gardens or nearby farms, to special events in our lives. The first peas of the year are one treat; so is a strawberry-rhubarb pie from Bonnie's strawberries, or our annual family gathering at Thanksgiving, with each bringing our specialties. It is these relationships between food and eater, carried back to the farm, that could form the basis of a truly sustainable cuisine. If widely acted upon, they would challenge the very basis of our current agricultural economy.

We are beginning to see, in small ways, that individual decisions to make these connections are having an impact. I can speak most directly about the changes in Maine. Thirty years ago, most farmers produced bulk foods for wholesale markets. Rural communities usually had a farm stand or two; there were two, barely surviving, farmers' markets in the State. Now nearly every major town has both a farmers' market and an independent natural food store or cooperative; most leading restaurants seek out local foods in season for their menu. Hundreds of Maine farmers now provide organic food to a growing number of citizens.

The idea of producing regionally distinctive foods is also taking hold, with farmstead cheese makers, smoked seafood, and specialty potato varieties. We even have farmers turning the seasons on their head, producing cool season salad greens in unheated greenhouses during the Fall, Winter, and early Spring, using far less energy than produce imported from afar. Long-term relationships with customers are the key to survival for many farmers, small and large. The most direct linkages are the Community Supported Agriculture (CSA) projects, where farmers and buyers make commitments to one another ahead of the production season. At that level, where consumers and farmers are interacting and talking, I am optimistic.

I'd like to propose two strategies that can help to rebuild connections between the person eating the food, and the person growing the food. The first is based on thinking about "face, place, and taste" as explicit components of a sustainable cuisine. The Japanese have a word for it, seikatsu, meaning "food with a face."

My favorite example of this comes from my great-uncle Arthur, who has been farming on the family homestead his whole life, and just now is slowing down as he moves through his eighties. He made his living selling feeder pigs, but recently sold all but one, left behind because his brother and sister needed a place to take their slops. He also sold his sheep, but he still keeps beef cows, chickens, and a big garden. Every time you visit you have a choice between something fresh from the garden, or something Arthur has put up in the kitchen. Recently my uncle Bob passed on samples of Arthur's pickles, along with the recipes. Arthur couldn't remember who'd given him the recipe, so he named it after the donor's hometown, and now "Wytopitlock Man Salt Pickles" has entered our family's repertoire, and diet. It has all the elements of sustainable cuisine: there is a face (actually several, besides my own family's: Uncle Bob, Great-uncle Arthur, and the man from Wytopitlock who gave him the recipe); there is a place (our Three Sisters Farm, the Libby family homestead); and, finally, there is a distinctive taste. Once you've tried Uncle Arthur's Wytopitlock Man Salt Pickles you either love them or you hate them, but you certainly remember them.

The second part of the strategy will require us to make this philosophy a part of our buying. We can start modestly here, but the potential is huge. A few years ago I roughly figured the potential impact on the very local economy of Mount Vernon if every household spent a small part of their food bill each week on products from the farms here: milk, meat, eggs, raspberries, vegetables, and sweet corn. Now I tell people that if each family in Maine spent $10 per week on local foods, it would create an additional $100 million in business and require three times as much fruit and vegetable production. Even in my small town of Mount Vernon, population 1,400, the difference would require a new full-time vegetable farming business.

When we can attach a face, a place, and a taste to our daily meals, and our institutions have evolved to encourage that interaction, then we will be sure we have achieved a truly sustainable cuisine. I think it looks a lot like supper during the gardening season.

Criteria for a Sustainable Cuisine

Annemarie Colbin, MA, CHES

Natural Gourmet Cooking School
48 West 21st Street
New York, NY 10010
www.naturalgourmetschool.com
www.foodandhealing.com

❧

Food, as Ralph Nader once wrote, is the most intimate consumer product. Each and every human being needs to eat at least two or more times per day. The food humans consume must serve as fuel, as disease-preventor, and be pleasant to the taste. Well-nourished human beings are resistant to infection and disease, contribute to society, and enjoy all the days of their lives.

Sustainable cuisine means that:

- Our food production can be sustained year after year,

- Local and seasonal food production is encouraged and supported,

- The foods we choose to eat take up no more of the earth's resources than absolutely necessary,

- Our daily food is of maximum nutrient density,

- Our cuisine is devoid of artificial and imitation substances that pass for food.

The daily choices we make at the marketplace, based on taste and nutritional choice, trickle upward to the food producers and distributors and give them information about what the public wants.

This is the type of "grassroots" movement that has so dramatically pushed forward the movement of organic agriculture. However, the food producers and distributors make choices of their own that trickle downward, and these choices are usually in support of their financial objectives. Two major examples are irradiation and genetic engineering, both of which are strongly rejected by the public, antithetical to sustainable cuisine, and yet pushed onto the marketplace by powerful corporations who want to sell their products regardless of their health effects.

Particularly obnoxious is the insidious silent growth of genetically engineered foods, which benefit no one but the large corporations that make them. Genetically engineered crops have grown so fast and so silently that the general public has almost no choice, and is unable to avoid them should they wish to do so. Techniques such as the "terminator seeds" and other "trademarked" seeds work completely against sustainability, as the farmers are obliged to buy new seeds every year.

The terminator seeds make plants that do not reproduce. Farmers are forbidden to keep "trademarked" seeds from one season to another or else they'll be charged with copyright infringement or "violating the license agreement," because they get a "license" to plant the seeds.

Nothing is further from sustainability. Should the corporation meet with some misfortune such as an earthquake or other disaster that disrupts or eliminates its operations, many thousands of farmers would be left without seeds and consequently, the food supply would be in dire straits. Our current agribusiness trend is unsustainable.

In fact, sustainable cuisine is my business. For the past twenty five years I have taught a simple set of criteria for healthy food selection. I founded a school on these principles, The Natural Gourmet Cookery School in New York City, which is licensed by the New York State Education Department. This is the only natural foods cooking school in the country that offers a Chef's Training Program in natural foods and health-supportive cuisine. My books, *The Book of Whole Meals*, *The Natural Gourmet*, *Food and Healing* (all from Ballantine Books) and *Food and Our Bones: The Natural Way to Prevent Osteoporosis*

(Dutton/Plume), all espouse these principles.

In my consulting practice, my lectures and speaking engagements, and my magazine columns for *Free Spirit* (New York) and *Natural Parent* (Great Britain), I always come back to these principles.

The Seven Criteria for Healthful (read Sustainable) Food Selection suggest that we choose food that is:

1. Whole—with all its natural edible parts: the whole grain with the bran and germ (not white pasta or bread, not refined cereals or sugar), as well as beans and legumes, vegetables, fruits, nuts, seeds—to be about 80% of our diet.

2. Fresh and Natural—minimally processed, without chemical additives, not canned or frozen or irradiated (read labels): "if it doesn't sound like food, it ain't food."

3. Real—no imitation color, flavor, artificial sweeteners, fake fats, or such.

4. Local, Seasonal, Organically Grown or Raised—supporting small farmers in our surrounding environment is a major assurance of sustainability and the availability of a healthful food supply for succeeding generations.

5. Traditional—foods that have been used for thousands of years, not "the latest" or "the newest."

6. Balanced—a dietary system that encompasses a wide variety of unprocessed foods of different types and colors—green, red, yellow, white vegetables and fruits, beans, whole grains and breads, nuts and seeds, some animal foods such as organic eggs, fowl, meats, fresh fish, wild game, and so on.

7. Delicious—fresh real foods are naturally flavorful, and should be prepared in the most nutrient-conserving and delicious way.

These criteria are fad-proof, and can be used any-where, any time, and in any part of the world. They allow for a vegetarian as well as a non-vegetarian lifestyle. They are broad enough to encompass all traditional and native cuisine.

These are the principles I follow to choose food for myself and my family. My children are now grown, but this is the type of food I raised them on, and they still follow the system. There may be times when one or more of the principles cannot be fol-lowed, such as when eating out. However, good restaurants offer free-range fowl and meats, fresh fish, fresh vegetables, salads, soups, and herbal teas, so more often than not, this is the way we eat. Also, it is easy to follow these criteria when trav-eling to other countries, and when partaking of multicultural cuisine.

Following the principles of sustainable cuisine will be good for people's health. However, if everyone suddenly stopped eating canned, frozen, and chemically enhanced foods, this could cause some disruption in the food system of our society. I do not see this happening in the near future. Nevertheless, the interest in fresh, whole, wholesome, organic, and real foods continues to increase, and more and more people count on getting their nourishment from them. I hope to see this sustainable trend move on to become the mainstream, and let the refined, colored, flavored, fake, artificial, and genetically engineered foods be a small minority of what human beings eat.

———o૪૪o———

On Achieving Sustainable Seafood Cuisine

Jerry R. Schubel, President & CEO
New England Aquarium

Roger Berkowitz, President & CEO
Legal Seafoods Restaurants

New England Aquarium
Central Wharf, Boston, MA 02110
www.neaq.org

Legal Seafoods
33 Everett Street, Allston, MA 02134
www.legalseafoods.com.
ᕔ

We hear a lot about sustainability these days. Sustainable development, sustainable agriculture, sustainable fisheries, sustainable tourism, and now, sustainable cuisine.

Perhaps nowhere does "sustainable cuisine" have more relevance than when it comes to the idea of "sustainable seafood cuisine." We use the term seafood to refer to both salt-water plants and animals and to fresh water plants and animals.

Seafood is among the best sources of protein available. It also can supply omega-3 oils, which have been shown to reduce the risk of cardiovascular disease. Doctors recommend that every adult eat fish at least once a week, and that those with a history of coronary disease eat fish twice a week. Seafood appears to be an excellent candidate for sustainable cuisine, but there is a problem.

If all of us in the US were to follow our doctors' advice and eat seafood even once a week, the consumption of seafood in the US would increase by somewhere between two and four times current levels. Since approximately two-thirds of all major marine fish stocks already are fished at, or above, sustainable levels, our approach to achieving sustainable marine fisheries needs to be redefined.

At the present rate, fish stocks will not provide a source of protein on a continuing basis even at present levels of harvest. Indeed, many stocks have already crashed and some fisheries have been severely curtailed or eliminated entirely to give the stocks a chance to rebuild. And, the effects are not restricted to the species caught and removed. The effects of the removal of many species of fish are transmitted throughout marine and fresh water food webs. Humans are not the only animals that enjoy seafood. Some animals depend upon it for their existence.

To sustain wild stocks of marine fishes, we need to develop effective management strategies and have the courage to enforce them. They must be multi-species management strategies because of the interdependence of species. They must be cross-jurisdictional because many species migrate and fail to recognize and respect human jurisdictional boundaries. And, there must be quotas on the number of fish taken—whether by limiting the catch or the catchers—and spawning, nursery, and other ecologically important areas need to be managed by periodic openings and closings to allow for renewal, much the way we do with crop rotation on land.

In addition, to achieve sustainable seafood cuisine to meet the growing demands for seafood, mariculture needs to be expanded significantly. But, more of the same kinds of mariculture is not the answer.

Mariculture operations need to be designed, sited, and executed carefully to avoid habitat destruction, to minimize pollution, to minimize conflicts with other important uses and values of marine areas, and to balance selective breeding and genetic manipulation in efforts to develop disease-resistant and rapidly-growing strains with appropriate attention to maintaining genetic diversity. It is clear that a sustainable seafood cuisine strategy will require far more knowledge, imagination, commitment and cooperation in management of wild fisheries and of mariculture than have characterized efforts to date.

Sophisticated consumers are one element in an over-all strategy.

The definition of sustainable cuisine suggests to us how theming of restaurants could contribute to this sense of sustainable cuisine. Restaurateurs need to be certain that they buy only from suppliers whose produce comes from sustainable sources. Menus should state where the seafood came from, and how they were grown and harvested. The New England Aquarium and Legal Seafoods have been leaders in these efforts.

Legal Seafoods buys only from suppliers who harvest from sustainable fisheries and they feature conservation information on their menus and on table tent cards. Legal Seafoods and the New England Aquarium have demonstrated that end users—retailers and restaurateurs—have a unique opportunity to educate the public. The fact that some species are not as abundant as others is also reflected in pricing.

In spite of the care the New England Aquarium exercises in the selection of seafood on its menu, this has not stopped us from being featured in the *Wall Street Journal* and on all the major television networks for the perceived conflict of having fish in its tanks and on its menu. We do not find these to be in contradiction. We are committed not only to sustainable fisheries, but also to sustainable fishing communities. New England fishing villages are important to the sense of place that makes New

England distinctive and that make it a tourist desti-nation. As we become a more global society—one in which tourism is the world's largest industry—authenticity will be a major driving force in sus-tainable tourism. Integral parts of New England's authenticity are its fishing communities and its seafood restaurants. The New England Aquarium's mission is "to present, promote, and protect the world of water." It is implicit that this mission extends to all the creatures that live in the world of water and all those that depend upon it.

There are opportunities to celebrate success stories, such as the farming of shrimp. Shrimp is not only more abundant now than a decade or so ago, but is more affordable than ever before. But, here, too, the sustainability record is mixed. In some parts of the world ecologically valuable mangrove swamps have been drained, filled and manipulated to create shrimp farms. The intentional destruction of natural habitat used as spawning and nursery areas for wild fish takes its toll on these stocks.

The case for salmon is more compelling, but even it is not without its critics. Over twenty-five years ago, salmon were abundant on the East Coast of the United States. Wild salmon are available now in significant numbers only in parts of the Pacific Northwest and in parts of Western Europe. The Norwegians saw an opportunity and started farming salmon. The industry spread to Chile, Scotland,

Ireland, Canada, and the United States (Maine). Today there is an abundance of salmon, consumption is at an all-time high, and prices are moderate. This farmed alternative to wild salmon has allowed the Alaskan wild stock not only to rebound, but to develop the cachet of being among the most flavorful of all fish.

Unfortunately, and surprising as it may seem, one of the major hurdles in luring the public away from the more popular and over-fished species such as cod and haddock, and transferring that demand to more abundant stocks often is tightly coupled to a product's name. Take wolffish or cusk, for example. Admittedly, in their whole, natural freshly caught state, wolffish and cusk are not very attractive, but once filleted, they lose their identity and are appealing. And, they taste good. The problem of marketability lies entirely in their names. Neither wolffish or cusk sounds particularly appetizing. A "Big Mac" might be less appealing if it were a called a "Big McGround Elsie the Cow" or a "Big McFat."

When New Zealanders and Australians discovered a fish occupying a habitat at about a mile in depth and that had a face—indeed an entire head—that only a mother could love, a head covered with cracks and crevices, an enterprising Australian marketer coined the name "orange roughy." Today the species is found on menus all over the world! Indeed, the strategy worked so well that this slowly reproducing fish is now badly over-fished. It seems that even ugliness is no defense against those who have to have their fish.

One of the best approaches to a sustainable seafood cuisine is to target some of the most popular species for aggressive aquaculture production. Today, serious efforts are underway to farm haddock and cod. Projects focusing on fluke (winter flounder) and summer flounder are starting to show rewards. In fact, Legal Seafoods will be involved in a summer program which aims to offer farmed product on its menu within the next 12 months! Other species under development are grey sole and halibut.

In closing, as two who depend upon fish for our livelihoods—one to display them and one to feature them on the menu—we are reminded of a quote from the famous Baltimore curmudgeon and journalist, the late H. L. Mencken: "For every problem, there is a simple solution—neat, plausible, and wrong." Achieving sustainable seafood cuisine is no exception.

———∞———

Sustainable Cuisine from the Garden

Gregory Long, President

The New York Botanical Garden
200th Street and Kazimiroff Boulevard
Bronx, NY 10458-5126
www.nybg.org

෴

The concept of sustainability is entirely central to the survival of our species, and it is a subject that the scientists, horticulturists, and educators at The New York Botanical Garden take very seriously.

We view sustainable cuisine as inseparably linked with the conservation of plant resources, which are the raw ingredients of many current and potentially sustainable sources of foods. Before any research institution can assist with the complex task of sustaining a plant resource, it must first know as much about the resource as possible. At the Garden, we accomplish this through an integrated, program of field and laboratory research. We are fully committed to collaborating with other scientific organizations, indigenous people, governmental agencies, industry, and resource managers from around the world to gather and share knowledge of these resources with the goal of ensuring their continued survival.

A Chinese proverb says that the first step on the path to wisdom is knowing things by their right names. Inspired by this credo, Garden scientists begin the research process in the field where they collect plants from diverse geographical areas around the world, ranging from the Intermountain region of the western United States to the highlands of Peru and the Amazonian basin. Back at their 250-acre campus in the Bronx, the Garden's scientists study, classify, describe, and name these plants. They publish information on their findings of plant relationships, distribution, utility, and sustainability. They even use DNA analysis in their laboratories to decipher the details of plants' properties and potential uses, be it for fuel, fibers, medicines, or foods. The data derived from this process serve as the basis of all subsequent plant research, and constitute the essential first step for any conservation effort.

Two of the Garden's current research projects on edible plants of global importance underscore the institution's role in documenting the diversity of food plants. In one example, Dr. Scott Mori and his collaborators study the diversity, ecology, and economic uses of plants in the Brazil nut family in northern South America. Their research has revealed the intricate relationships between the plants and their pollinators and agents of dispersal. They have concluded that the sustained availability and profitability of Brazil nuts depend greatly on the conservation of the forests in and around where they grow.

In another example, Dr. Michael Nee has documented the origin and diversification of the domesticated species of the genus Cucurbita, which includes the economically important squashes, gourds, and pumpkins. Dr. Nee traced these species to their origins in South and Central America, providing future investigators with clues for finding the location of populations of ancestral wild species. These ancestral species represent a storehouse of genetic diversity that can be used to breed new cultivars for agricultural production.

Collecting baseline data on a useful plant species is only the first step in assuring that it can be used sustainably. The next step is determining how this species is grown or harvested, who uses it and for what, and how it is valued. The Garden's economic botanists study exactly these sorts of questions, and they have focused their research on traditional methods of agriculture in the tropics. They have undertaken pioneering work on the study of non-timber forest resources with the express aim of strengthening the economic position of traditional cultures while promoting the conservation of the plants that sustain them.

One such study was Dr. Charles Peters' work on three species of edible fruits harvested from wild plants growing in the flooded forests of Peruvian Amazonia. These fruits—camu-camu, sacha mangua, and uvos—are highly valued locally but little known outside of their native region. Dr. Peters studied the density, annual growth, and fruit production of these species in their native forests. He then used market prices to approximate the value of these fruits in a section of standing forest—demonstrating for the people of the region that there are economically viable alternatives to logging.

While conserving forests and wild sources of food is essential, it would be naive to think that we could harvest all the food we need from untouched forests. Dr. Christine Padoch is an anthropologist at the Garden who has studied a complex method of raising economic plants in the tropics called "swidden-fallow management." This method of agriculture involves cutting and burning small sections of forests, planting and harvesting useful plants until their yield declines, and then moving on to a different section of forest that had been left fallow years before. Indigenous peoples have practiced this cyclical management technique for many generations with very little overall impact on the forest. Swidden-fallow management is a sustainable alternative to the highly destructive clear cutting and establishment of cattle pastures practiced by "modern" land managers.

Doing research is just one of the duties of Garden scientists. When scientists return from a trip, they publish their research in scientific and popular articles. They also may share their findings with teachers in the Garden's education department. Using original research and other sources of information, the Garden and its scientists educate consumers about sustainable cuisine.

People who take classes through The New York Botanical Garden's Continuing Education Program, such as "Ethnobotany of the Amazon" or "Ethnobotany of the Nightshades," or attend lectures like "Managing the Tropical Rainforest" or "Creating a Global Network," see firsthand the issues that affect the sustainability of food plants. They learn about the origins of the food they eat and see some alternatives to agribusiness and corporate forestry. Most importantly, they become aware of the complexity of resource management issues and may even begin to reexamine some of their own habits.

For people who are increasingly isolated from the production of the resources they consume, a trip to our Garden to observe important food plants can be an enlightening experience. Garden horticulturists grow many species of food plants both on the grounds and inside the Garden's Enid A. Haupt Conservatory. Horticulturists work closely with Garden scientists and educators to create an educational environment at the Garden. Interpretive signs and brochures produced by the Horticulture Division are integral to a visitor's educational experience, often inspiring further study.

SUSTAINABLE CUISINE

Although a swidden fallow in Amazonia might seem light years away from a restaurant in Manhattan, we at The New York Botanical Garden believe they are inextricably linked. As the world population grows and explosive development threatens biological and cultural resources, we must promote sustainability by forging creative partnerships with diverse parties, ranging from the local farmer to the corporate executive, and, ultimately, with the executive chef.

By educating ourselves we have taken the first step in achieving a truly sustainable cuisine. Informed customers will want a palm heart that is harvested sustainably, as opposed to a product that is "mined" from a species that does not resprout and perpetuate itself. Every expedition—and the Garden has sponsored more than 1,000 of them over a span of 100 years—brings back plant specimens and information that could lead to the discovery of new food sources. It is up to scientists, working with partners, to ensure that the discoveries are developed in such a way that the very resource itself does not become endangered due to overzealous harvesting. It is in this role that The New York Botanical Garden best contributes to the reality of a sustainable cuisine in the 21st century.

More Than
Food for Thought

Sarah Johnston

Northeast Organic Farming Association of New York
597 Route 9J
Stuyvesant, NY 12173
sjds@wizvax.net

From my perspective, sustainable agriculture is the foundation upon which sustainable cuisine rests. The issues related to sustainable agriculture —food safety, world food production (which may or may not be related to world hunger), the implications of global use of genetically modified plants, the ever-shrinking proportion of the food dollar that reaches the farmer, conventional agriculture's structural dependence on pesticides and herbicides, the deliberate vertical integration and consolidation of the food industry from seed to processed foods, the average number of miles food travels before being consumed, the continuing loss of prime agricultural farm land—all fall within the concept of sustainable cuisine.

Sustainable cuisine goes a step beyond this list of problems of the world and makes the work of agricultural advocacy groups seem less dreary.

Oh excellent food! Ideally, sustainable cuisine is the deliberate choice of organically and regionally grown, seasonally available vegetables, fruits, grains, dairy products and meats, prepared into delicious, delightful meals that nourish the body and spirit. With renowned chefs on the side of organic food producers, perhaps we will worry less and eat more!

Chefs, food professionals and good cooks dedicated to a sustainable cuisine are part of a growing network of people interested in healthy, high quality, locally grown foods. Advocates for locally grown, healthy foods can drive demand for organic food production. Sustainable cuisine can teach the nutritional and social wisdom of enjoying Russet potatoes and Buttercup squash in the dark days of December and waiting for the first luscious local strawberries in June, each variety with a taste as distinctive as a different wine.

Thoughtfully chosen, well-prepared food can win over hearts and minds to eating seasonally and enjoying the changes in foods that the seasons bring. Sustainable cuisine must step out of the restaurant and into people's homes with recipes that inspire people to prepare seasonally available produce. This is no small task. Farmers' markets have found it necessary to have cooking demonstrations to show people how to prepare the vegetables for sale.

Quality is a combination of plant variety, how the vegetables or fruits are grown, when they are picked, and how they are shipped. When crops are grown organically, people can be certain about how the crop was grown. Organic farming, according to the standards of the Northeast Organic Farming Association of New York and similar organizations around the country, is a method of sustainable agricultural production that is not dependent on pesticides and herbicides. Sustainable organic farming is a system that works within the principles of the natural world to grow crops, rather than attempting to grow crops despite what we know about the natural world. A simple example: insects and disease are frequently crop-specific, so organic growers rotate crops from one location to another. In this way, they break the cycle of insects or diseases that can get a foothold in soils in the first growing season and then reach damaging levels the next growing season. If the same crop is grown in the same location year after year, populations of insects and soil-borne disease continue to plague the crop.

Organic growing systems work because of healthy, living soils. Despite huge amounts of research and factual information, the mystery of the soil has yet to be well understood. Organic growers work with all the knowledge available and make very different choices than conventional farmers. Nitrogen, phosphorus and potassium, the three standard nutrients for plants, can be added to soils as soluble chemical fertilizers for quick release to plants. But the same properties that make these fertilizers immediately available to plants also make them pollutants in surrounding surface waters, groundwater and the air. These chemical infusions also change and deaden the microbiological soil community.

Organic farmers depend on the same three nutrients, but they use crushed rock for phosphorus and potassium, and then count on soils teeming with microorganisms to make the rock supplements available to plants on a much slower basis. Organic farmers typically add nitrogen by sowing nitrogen-fixing cover crops, plants on whose roots flourish symbiotic bacteria that fix nitrogen from the atmosphere and make it available to the growing crop. Plant residues from the cover crop are then turned under so the nitrogen can be used by the next crop in the rotation. Cover cropping also adds valuable organic matter to the soil, which is the dynamic force of organic growing systems.

Crops grown at the speed assigned by nature tend to be less susceptible to pests, more resistant to disease. In addition, they are more flavorful. Good farmers always know how their vegetables taste, and choose their varieties for flavor. Lettuces that grow well in the early part of the season are not the same varieties chosen to remain sweet in the heat of the summer. And the difference in the flavors of different varieties of tomatoes is remarkable. An August tomato tasting can be great fun but it can only happen in August. The only tomatoes I enjoy eating in January are those same August-ripe tomatoes, canned at the height of their sunny sweetness.

The most sought after assurance carried by organically grown foods is that they have been grown without the use of harmful pesticides. In the information war being waged in the press, companies that sell pesticides and herbicides would have us believe that we must continue to use these products in order to eat. This myth exists to sell products, not feed people. The battle to control information about food safety continues at the federal level with regard to product labels.

By limiting labeling, the U.S. Environmental Protection Agency and the Food and Drug Administration do not allow the consumer to distinguish between items that may contain controversial products. For example, rBGH, the recumbent bovine growth hormone approved for use in dairy cows in the US (and recently rejected for use in Canada and the European Union) may or may not be in the milk you drink, but US dairies wishing to distinguish their milk products are not allowed to label their product as rBGH-free. There is no labeling requirement for foods that contain genetically modified plants or animals. And the food industry is now fuming about the fact that USDA pesticide residue data on vegetables and fruits was publicized by Consumers Union.

No one should have to worry about toxins in foods, yet we all know we must worry today, so that tomorrow this fear can be eliminated. We must renew our efforts to make government decisions reflect the interests of individuals. We must also convince our government to set goals for domestic organic production and assist farmers in making the transition to sustainable methods of agricultural production, as several European countries have done.

Sustainable cuisine can add to the momentum of the sustainable agricultural movement by supporting the efforts of farmers growing organic foods sustainably and by advocating that food professionals and cooks in the home subscribe to a sensible approach to seasonal cooking. Food is one of the simple pleasures of life. Sustainable cuisine's challenge and gift is to incorporate all we think is important about agricultural production onto one delicious plate.

———⊗⊗⊗———

Sustainable Cuisine, Sustainable Agriculture

Jim Gardiner

Northeast Sustainable Agriculture
Research Education Program (NESARE)
University of Vermont
#10 Hills Building
Burlington, VT 05405-0082
www.uvm.edu/~nesare

◌

S ustainable cuisine means cooking with raw materials that were produced by farmers and others employing the precepts of sustainable agriculture. Sustainable agriculture calls for minimal use of pesticides, fertilizers, growth hormones, and other chemical inputs, because of concern for their effects on the environment and farmers—both are likely to suffer if chronically exposed to many of these substances. Depending on where you live, sustainable cuisine may mean looking for certain logos at the store, certifying, for instance, that fruit was grown according to the principles of IPM (integrated pest management). Some might expand the notion of sustainable cuisine to include ethical treatment of animals, as, for instance, certified on "dolphin-safe" cans of tuna.

Sustainable cuisine also has an economic aspect. It means recognizing that if farmers are to be kept in business, and farming sustained, they deserve a living wage for their efforts. This in turn may mean purchasing through unconventional channels, such as farmers' markets, or on-farm stands. Some florists and restaurants strike up deals with farmers for regular deliveries of custom-grown produce. This allows the customer to specify particular varieties, and to vary the mix with the season. Alternatively, the chefs in some restaurants construct their menus around what is available from the farmers with whom they deal. Such unconventional marketing returns more of the consumer's dollar to the farmer.

It probably does not occur to most people, when they look at the unblemished fruits and vegetables that fill the bins in the produce departments that this is not natural. It is difficult to grow produce that is perfectly shaped, free of worms, unchewed by caterpillars and other insects, without substantial application of pesticides. Sustainable cuisine, then, also means accepting something less than perfection in the appearance of raw produce, which after all can be made up for during preparation of the final product.

Sustainable agriculture, in its most general terms, means those practices that keep farmers farming, and keep rural communities that depend on the farm economy alive. It means long-term profitability, emphasis on the words "long-term," which implies in turn such matters as responsible stewardship of natural resources, and being a good neighbor. It also means maintaining the interest of the next generation in farming. In the area of pest control, sustainable agriculture means practicing IPM by, for instance waiting for pest populations to reach a certain threshold before spraying, or better yet, exploiting natural predators for pest control instead of spraying. Best of all, though, would be, through judicious use of rotations, cultivation, and attention to the soil, to prevent the problem from arising in the first place.

Sustainable agriculture gives particular attention to the soil. It stresses erosion control, soil ecology, and the importance of sustaining a high organic content. A well-nurtured, living soil can provide buffering against flood and drought, convert organic detritus to nutrients and hold these nutrients against leaching or run-off, extract free nitrogen from the air, improve the physical structure and till of the soil, and discourage disease and pest organisms. Sustainable agriculture means paying attention to the carbon balance in the soil, as well as the N, P, and K, of more traditional agriculture. Sustainable agriculture also means crop diversification. Monoculture, the opposite of diversification, is inherently unstable, as it can leave the prosperity of farms, communities, and even whole regions dependent on the market fluctuations of a single crop, and the vicissitudes of weather and pest incidence as they affect that crop. Diversification to avoid putting all one's eggs in the same basket is highly compatible with rotation for the purposes of maintaining soil fertility and controlling pests. Sustainable agriculture means showing respect for the environment and one's neighbors, by taking measures to avoid polluting public waters with pesticide residues, excess nutrients, and eroded soil. Where suburbs are encroaching on farmland, it may also include taking measures to control foul odors. If, after all, offended neighbors enact local ordinances whose effect is to make farming impracticable, agriculture will not have been sustained.

Above all, sustainable agriculture means a holistic approach to farming; a consideration of the farm as a totality; and an awareness that any farming practice may have unintended consequences. Sustainable agriculture means asking what else besides the target insect will be killed, before applying an insecticide, or whether salt build-up will result from irrigation, and what the long-term effects of that will be. No less important, it asks whether the purchase of these and other inputs will involve incurring an unbearable burden of debt.

In short, sustainable agriculture means solving problems without creating new ones.

The Chocolate Factor

The Organic Commodity Products, Inc.

29 Elm Street
Cambridge, MA 02139
ocp@shore.net

❧

The Organic Commodity Project, Inc. (OCP) was founded on the principal that agriculture can play a key role in environmental conservation.

OCP recognizes that sustainable agriculture, and its cousin, sustainable cuisine, can play an important role in stemming the loss of species, maintaining a stable local economy and enabling investment in the future through appropriate and sustainable land management techniques.

Why chocolate?

OCP chose to focus on cocoa, not only because we love taste testing, but because cocoa can be used as an "anchor" cash crop in a diversified agroforestry system.

Theobroma cacao is, by biological design, an understory tree—an underlying layer of vegetation—in humid tropical forests. It's aboriginal home consists of multi-layered forest systems with a diverse arboreal canopy providing shelter from intense sun and rain as well as providing nutritious leaf litter. A multi-layered forest system continues to be the optimum environment for its cultivation as well as, we would like to suggest, for its sustainable and commercial cultivation. Cocoa grown in this type of system holds enormous potential for environmental and cultural conservation in regions under intense pressure from logging, development and conventional, monocrop agriculture.

The cultivation conditions for what we can call "sustainable cocoa" include a multi-tiered, vertically diverse forest canopy with 40-70% shade density. This may not be primary growth rain forest but these conditions encourage and support organism diversity to move toward the restoration of a mature forest system. The benefits of this type of system include the attraction of beneficial insects for pest control, breeding opportunities for natural pollinators, and varieties of habitat for diverse populations of flora and fauna. The inputs required for organic cacao cultivation are minimal compared to conventional methods, reducing the expense and risk of using chemicals for the growers.

Any system developed for sustainable cocoa must be one which allows for high biodiversity while providing for farmers' subsistence and cash needs. Our experience has shown us that cocoa can be produced commercially in a biologically rich and diverse forest environment in the humid tropics. The humid tropics can also yield additional subsistence products for the farmer, such as fruits, medicines, spices, timber and building material, animals (protein), root crops and other materials. Some of these products may be additional cash crops as well. By having a sustained cash income through cocoa production the farmer is also able to meet other needs while providing the most sustainable habitat for cocoa production. Cocoa grown in this manner may also develop or maintain a strong immune system which will benefit the harvest and future plant generations.

Organic agriculture attempts to take into account the entire system in which the crops are grown. This prevents many of the problems that can result from input-heavy conventional agriculture. However, organic agriculture is not always synonymous with sustainable agriculture. OCP believes that any agriculture, even if it meets organic standards, that does not protect and support the living systems which are indigenous to its region is not sustainable. Organic standards do strive for sustainability but they do not require growers to achieve it.

In the example of our business, we work with producers who grow cocoa in situations that range from diverse poly-cultures to single species systems. It has taken several years to develop a market which will support this work. Consumers in US, European and Pacific Rim markets are beginning to recognize the value of diversified growing conditions through various certification labels being applied to consumer goods such as certified organic. Most cocoa grown in the world is not produced in diverse poly-cultures but rather in situations of full or partial sun which need restoration to approach a bio-diverse system. Specific knowledge of the desirable, or "reference," ecosystems is necessary to restore a growing region from environmental degradation back to ecological health. This process requires a long-term commitment and can take generations to achieve depending on the degree of devastation, even without political or financial barriers.

It is safe to say that OCP has just begun to address the multitude of challenges related to sustainable cocoa production. As our work pertains to sustainable cocoa production we have been able to, in the past four years:

- Identify and stimulate the demand for cocoa products using organic cocoa;

- Identify that strong extension support is critical to begin to meet sustainable goals;

- Create assessment and planning tools applicable to a wide variety of cocoa growing regions in light of the demand increase;

- Establish that the market may prove to be the critical link to stimulating sustainable production;

- Indicate that further region-specific research is necessary to identify sustainable production plans.

It is OCP's belief that sustainable cocoa production will not only lead to environmental integrity and social and economic stability, but will also improve productivity and supply security.

An assessment of the current environmental impact of cocoa production in key cocoa growing regions is an important step in identifying long term restorative strategies. The work will also be vital in determining what positive production schemes already exist. Furthermore, understanding that cocoa economies in the same regions will help identify what socioeconomic needs must be met.

Continued and rigorous research to support and identify sustainable cultivation techniques specific to each cocoa growing region will be a necessary and important ingredient in developing cross trade support for sustainable production. A good example of cross trade cooperation is the development of alternatives to methyl bromide for post harvest pest control. This specific research into safe pest control methods will become a key link in the chain of providing environmentally safe products.

One of the largest challenges that we have experienced is that of implementing good sound research. Coalitions of producers, governments, buyers, scientists and ultimately consumers will be required to see that the sound findings that will come out of continued research can be implemented without inflating costs unnecessarily.

Implementation techniques will vary region to region based on cultural, economic, political and financial pressures. The success of implementing appropriate research findings will ultimately fall on community level organizations because it is the farmers who are the land stewards.

Proactive market response to environmental degradation in cocoa growing regions will have a strong impact on stemming the tide of species and habitat loss. The response can come in the form of:

- Developing and marketing products that utilize cocoa growth in sustainable or restorative cultivation programs;

- Consumer education of the issues related to tropical environment degradation as well as the farmers economic challenges;

- Industry support and participation in research related to sustainable cocoa cultivation;

- Industry support of research implementation through extension programs and local farmers organizations.

We must, as an industry, be careful about the presentations and representations we make to the consumers of our products. Too many "pro-environment" and "social justice" labels can confuse consumers and weaken the overall messages. Any product using "good housekeeping" environment seals run the risk of weakening the industry's message of

corporate responsibility, product safety and environmental and social justice. If a consumer feels that an
OK environmental seal is a marketing ploy with no
respected certifying body behind it the consumer is
likely to not support the product. There remains
value at retail in cause related marketed products but
any seals or certification that speaks to the product's
environmental benefits must be backed up by a real-
istic and legitimate implementation program.

Legislation is a critical component to insuring
regional implementation of sustainable initiatives. In
some cocoa producing countries there may be barriers to supporting farmer's sustainable cocoa production. It is important that each cocoa growing region
establish legislative initiatives that insure farmers'
rights to their crops and to manage the land that they
grow on in a sustainable way through secure land
tenure. Because restorative practices may require
many years to develop real results it is critical that
growers are provided with incentives to invest time
and effort into their land through ownership security.

Finally, growers must be assured that any premiums
paid for sustainable cocoa to marketing bodies are
also passed on to them. Economic stability is at the
core of this issue. We also believe that economic stability is an important part of a viable definition of
sustainable cuisine.

———∞———

Sustainable Cuisine is Organic Cuisine

Bob Scowcroft

Organic Farming Research Foundation
P.O. Box 440
Santa Cruz, CA 95061
http://www.ofrf.org

꙳

The future of our environment depends upon an informed consumer, and the development of "sustainable cuisine."

Because of the impact a food purchase has on our land, air, water and oceans, the consumer's right to know is vital. Through the use of eco-labels many different organizations have attempted to inform the consumer that what they are eating is environmentally sound and sustainably produced. However, only one term has the force of state and federal labeling law behind it—Certified Organically Grown and/or Processed.

Certified organic refers to products that have been grown and processed according to strict uniform standards, verified annually by independent state or private organizations. Certification includes inspection of farm fields and processing facilities. The USDA is now in the process of developing federal standards for organic foods. When a set of guidelines is finally approved and implemented, all organic foods will be required to be certified and meet these national standards. This will cover all organic crops and processed foods, including produce, grains, meat, dairy, eggs and fiber.

Organic farming systems do not use chemical pesticides or fertilizers. Instead, they are based on the development of biological diversity and the maintenance and replenishment of soil fertility. Organic foods are minimally processed to maintain the integrity of the food without artificial ingredients, preservatives, genetically modified organisms or irradiation.

Organic farmers' primary strategy in controlling pests and diseases is prevention. Organic farmers build healthy soils; this produces healthy plants that are better able to resist disease and insect predation. Organic farmers also rely on a diverse population of soil organisms, insects, birds, and other organisms to keep pests in check. Weeds are controlled through increased cultivation and crop rotation. Organically raised livestock are fed organic feed and allowed free range and outdoor access; they are not given antibiotics, hormones, or medications in the absence of illness.

In 1997, organic products represented over $4.2 billion

in retail sales, or 1% of the US food supply. Sales of organic products have increased by at least 20% annually over the past six years. While the organic industry has grown steadily, the development of technical expertise to support it has fallen behind. In proving the success of organic agriculture, organic farmers have had to rely upon one another for research and information exchange. By and large, all information regarding the production and sales of organic food products comes from non-governmental sources or the trade association that serves this emerging industry.

Fostering a grower-based information system is at the heart of the Organic Farming Research Foundation's mission. In pursuit of this mission, OFRF conducts a competitive grant-making program to support organic farming research and education, and engages policy-makers in an effort to increase the funding and scope of publicly supported organic farming research. We're working to ensure a secure future for family farmers producing safe, nutritious food and contributing to a healthier natural environment for all of us. While we support the concept of ecological food labeling, only one term guarantees the right to know how your food was grown and processed and that is certified organically grown and/or processed.

Eating Sustainably, What You Can Do

Organic Valley/CROPP Cooperative

306 North East Holman Street
Portland, OR 97211
www.organicvalley.com

W hen we think of the word sustainable here at Organic Valley, we think of honoring the interdependency of all life and understanding the carrying capacity of the earth. This reflects our stated mission as organic producers as well as our spiritual and emotional ideals. How does this translate in the kitchen? What role does this play in fulfilling the basic need of feeding oneself to survive?

Let's face it. The word cuisine connotes "art"—the art of marrying flavors to produce exquisite sensations for the palate. Most of us don't just simply eat to live. Food has become "cuisine," making a simple pleasure from a day-to-day event. The choices we make daily to fulfill this "simple" pleasure have broad-reaching effects, not always positive. To create a truly sustainable cuisine, we must add more criteria to our concept of quality: the environmental and social-cultural impact of food production. Important questions—how was this food produced, this animal raised, this food handled—must be added to the list defining quality cuisine. These practices do affect flavor, quality, nutrition, the environment, our quality of life, and the world at large.

It takes little research to discover that agriculture has been an environmental culprit for 2000 years or more. Consider the cedars of Lebanon, a legendary forest now a desert. Here at home, thousands of tons of topsoil are lost to the Gulf of Mexico annually, Midwest water wells are contaminated, the FDA is concerned about antibiotic use in livestock production, and Consumer Reports and the National Academy of Science report our children may be at risk due to pesticides. Statistics on farm worker miscarriages provided such testimony years ago.

So what is sustainable cuisine? It's making choices based on knowing—where your food comes from; how it is grown, packaged and processed—and using that knowledge to make the best choices possible. Information is key here. You may not know that your favorite French fries are grown in a highly irrigated desert, subsidized by your taxes, sprayed 12 times per year to fight blights. Most probably, the seed is genetically modified, a special hybrid owned by a multinational corporation, bred especially to a certain size so the potato can be peeled and sliced with automation. These fries, after cooking, hang nicely over the takeout container, creating the visual appeal that most certainly makes them taste and sell better. Furthermore, these French fries go out in truck and container loads all over the world, replacing hundreds of local varieties in unlikely places like Russia, China and Peru.

So the question should really be, is it possible for the majority of Americans to eat sustainably? Americans now spend less than 11¢ of every dollar on food— compared to 18–21¢ in most developed countries.

Consumers have grown used to spending very little on their food, and asking very few questions. This makes promoting sustainable cuisine challenging.

Luckily, we all have choices, if we are informed enough to understand them. Eating sustainably requires that we go the extra mile to understand how our food is grown and where it comes from. It can't be reduced to one practice or one issue. It's not just about pesticides, for example, or recycling. Our cuisine must be regarded like a farm, with an emphasis on understanding interdependency, the whole picture, from cradle to grave, from soil to package to table. No choice is perfect, but there are better choices.

Here is the common list of considerations:

The best choice is generally to buy local, certified organic if it is available. Organic production is notorious for its stringent attitude toward food production. If it's local and one knows the farmer and something about his production practices, that is a very good choice. Sustaining farm families living nearby is without question valuable. Next, variety is an important component of flavor and suitability to the region. Do we really want a world where only five varieties of corn exist, all patented by large corporations? Are red delicious apples really suitable for every region, every climate? Look and ask for regional varieties of all fresh produce and meats. Look for products in season when choosing all fresh food. These choices are bound to be freshest and tastiest. And, of course, there is the whole arena of packaging and processing and the impact these food choices have on health and the environment. Minimal processing and packaging are generally best, as we know. Neither should we ignore the more complex issues of the social-cultural impact of what we eat in this discussion. Rows of trailers for underpaid workers have replaced the family farm in the livestock industry. We are turning over our agriculture to huge corporations and immense factory farms that use chemicals and confinement predominantly. This type of cuisine clearly has hurt our soil, our rural communities, the livability of our cities and the overall quality of our food. Although we constantly hear the argument that this type of agriculture is necessary to feed the world, there is a mounting body of evidence favoring just the opposite position. The "green" revolution of the '60s has driven family farmers out of business all over the world. Starvation is still a problem in many nations.

The social-cultural issues surrounding farming are very important ones affecting our business at Organic Valley/CROPP Cooperative. Our farms are intentionally small and run by families. We choose national marketing because of efficiency, but strive for local production when it makes sense.

Hence we have farmers on both coasts and in-between—ten states in total. As an organic farmers' cooperative, every aspect of sustainable food production drives the decisions we make—from variety to appropriate scale of production to packaging. Our vegetable producers look for unusual varieties; our dairy farmers favor breeds that thrive on pasture. We consistently reach out to consumers to share our practices and philosophy with them. Organic, sustainable production is 100% in harmony with what we want for our company, our communities, our health, our animals, our earth and our cuisine.

Consumers spend as much as $8 billion per week on their cuisine, just in the US! It can't be said too often, the consumer votes in the marketplace every time she/he spends a dollar. Focusing these purchases toward the best sustainable choices can and does change the world!

———⊗◊⊗———

Earth Friendly Wine

Organic Wine Company

1592 Union Street, Number 350
San Francisco, CA 94123
www.ecowine.com

Since 1980, we have imported a selection of the finest certified organic wines available. They come from our family property and from about a dozen other excellent organic wine producers in France & Italy. All of the wines are Earth-friendly, made in partnership with nature from certified organically grown grapes. They are free of pesticides, herbicides, chemical fertilizers and other synthetic chemicals, and essential natural preservatives like sulfur dioxide are kept to a minimum. In the cellar, modern and traditional techniques are combined, producing the best possible wines with the fewest detrimental effects on the environment. Grapes are often picked by hand and the wine made gently, with minimal handling and filtration.

As we approach the new millennium, there is no question, our natural resources are limited and our environment is fragile. High yield conventional farming techniques continue to poison plants, soil, wildlife and people. 1.25 billion pounds of agricultural chemicals are applied to crops each year in the US alone. Conventionally grown grapes are one of the most heavily sprayed. Studies show that 17 different insecticides, herbicides and fumigants are used in wine production, many containing possible carcinogens. Our health, and the health of our planet, is at stake.

We believe that the system of organic agriculture, where healthy and productive soils develop quality crops without the use of synthetic chemicals, is the key to building our agricultural future. Every time you buy organically, you are supporting a philosophy that extends much further than your own table. The idea of organic agriculture has continued to develop and has rapidly expanded in the past few decades. Sales of organic foods totaled $78 million in 1980, but jumped to $4 billion in 1997. More and more, people are looking towards organic products, and supply is steadily increasing to meet demand. Chefs embrace organic foods for their appearance and taste, and by example are influencing consumers to do the same.

———∞∞∞———

Sustainable Omnivores

Phyllis Passariello

Associate Professor of Anthropology, Program Chair
Centre College
West Walnut Street
Danville, KY 40422
www.centre.edu

❧

Omnivore. We are omnivores: we eat it all, or at least, supposedly we can. But is our ability to eat it all a right, a privilege, or simply a residual predilection of our evolutionary story?

Given a free choice, humans choose a diet high in protein, salt, sugar and fat. Fast Food triumphs. But once again, we run up against the anthropological cliché—that humans are designed for a life of nomadic foraging, not sedentary lounge-lizarding nor couch-potato-ing. We are designed to be strolling around finding and eating nuts, roots, and berries, not driving to pick-up windows for burgers, shakes, and fries. In the wild, the veld, the forest, the jungle, luxury foods, especially sugars and fats, are rare treats and valuable nutritional necessities because of their rarity. Our bad backs, big guts, high cholesterol and clogged arteries attest to the long-term maladaptation, despite short-term pleasures, of our rich food choices. And rich, rico, cher at whose expense?

Anthropologists Sidney Mintz *(Sweetness and Power)* and Marvin Harris *(Good to Eat)* allude respectively to the "power" of sugar as a luxury food as well as an economically and politically loaded commodity, and to the "power" of meat in the human quest for protein and seemingly optimal survival strategies. Issues of global capitalism and related oppressions are relevant here. Are we to remain culturally relative (I'm OK and you're OK, even if you are stuffing your face while others languish) and politically correct instead of viable, just, humane world citizens?

Are there recipes, solutions for these excesses? Can we look beyond an illusory past, a Golden Age when life was simple, men were men, or at least boys were boys, and girls were nice, tidy, and knew how to cook? How do we, the middle class, white eggheads, explain our own conscious attempts to exercise regularly and eat a healthful, "Mediterranean" diet? Are we striving to become wanna-be suburban peasants with our masks of moderation covering our sins of conscious overindulgence, albeit of a more subtle variety? As a consumer of designer foods myself, I don't have any answers. I simply sit at the table and learn to love my radicchio.

Comfort foods demand our attention anthropologi-
cally and even politically. In very informal surveys, I
have established to my own satisfaction that, perhaps
even cross-culturally, comfort foods are generally
pale, mushy, warm, and rather bland. (For example,
mashed potatoes, hot cream of wheat, macaroni and
cheese, cream of chicken soup, etc.) Comfort foods
appear to be a retro throwback to mother's milk and
pablum. From another angle, comfort foods parallel
cross-culturally so-called staples in a variety of diets.
Staples include foods such as rice, millet, manioc,
potatoes, corn, wheat (bread). What is the staple in
our culture? Hard to say. Maybe it used to be bread,
but now, bread is simply a vehicle within which to
hold our true staple: flesh (meat, fish, etc.). Of
course, these protein overloads ultimately turn out to
be the foods of dis-comfort and dis-ease, nutritionally,
psychically, politically. (Pause: got to stop to pop
a few cashews here. Nobody's perfect—imperfection
is the definition of human!)

So finally, what are, what can be sustainable foods for
our world? We are beyond, in population and history,
a time of Eden's bounty. There is no going back. We
have to construct our own neo-Eden. But, is the
point of sustainable food to sustain us or the foods?
Both. All. The system. The logic of sustainability is
in the logic of holistic world ecology. We have to
educate and nurture our omnivorousness.

Personally, I do have a small step, a little answer:

soup. Looking again cross-culturally, we see comfort foods/staples jazzed up, herbed and spiced and even disguised into what might be called cosmic soup(s). Whether enhanced with matzo balls, slivers of pork and bean sprouts, lentils, noodles or simply a blend of hot water, fat and salt, a bowl of soup goes a long way—nutritionally, psychically, and politically.

From my Italian American family of great cooks and picky eaters, I am suggesting soup as an item of sustainable cuisine. To quote myself (from: *Eating Culture: The Italian Yankee Cookbook—An Ethnographic Reminiscence*, Altrimenti: 1997): "Hearty Stews and Soups—This section might be called soul-y as well as hearty since it includes the heart and soul of our childhood cuisine. New World peasantry thrived on these filling and surprisingly healthy dishes, which are now enjoying a comeback, due to the new 'colon' awareness, shall we say, as well as the anti-quiche and croissant yuppie backlash *(p. 41)*."

"Minestre—This is usually a hearty winter dish, but can also be made in the spring with fresh dandelions pulled out from your own lawn...All that 'minestre' really means in Italian is 'something that is soupy;' in our family, minestre means 'beans and greens.' To be served with Farina Rossa (recipe follows), usually broken in pieces and added to your bowl."

Minestre

1 can cannelli beans
  (or make white beans from scratch)

3 lbs escarole (dandelions...)

2 cloves garlic

  salt, pepper

1 ham bone

1 Tbs minced salt pork (optional)

2 Tbs olive oil
  (more if vegetarian, omit meats above)

Simmer hambone in water. Wash and steam greens, saving about one cup of liquid. Set aside. Brown minced salt pork in olive oil. Add escarole and saute. Add hambone and liquid to escarole. Add can of beans. If too thick, add water set aside from escarole steaming earlier. Simmer for about 5 minutes. *Serve. (With Farina Rossa)*

Farina Rossa

We are unable to determine why this is called "farina rossa" (which translates as "red wheat," while the corn meal used is yellow).

1 and _ cups yellow corn meal

  (approximately, judge by consistency)

1 Tbs olive oil

  salt, pepper

1 cup water

Boil water with olive oil, salt and pepper. Add corn meal in steady stream, stirring constantly. Cook until very dry, about 5 minutes at least. Put in small baking dish that has been oiled. Bake at 400 degree oven for about 30 minutes. *(pp. 46 –48)*

Working Conclusion:

Holistic New World corn and beans, Old World olive oil and garlic, mixed with "Other"-worldly common sense. The key to sustainable cuisine is a seeming simplicity, which is, simultaneously, a savvy intuition, a cultural memory, a human predilection for sustaining ourselves as informed and adaptive omnivores. We, the human species, can learn from ourselves.

⸺∞⸺

Sustainable Cuisine Must Be Pesticide Free

Pesticide Action Network North America

49 Powell Street, Suite 500
San Francisco, CA 94102
www.panna.org

Pesticides are not only hazardous to human health and the environment, but there is evidence that due to such factors as insect and weed resistance, they are counterproductive in the long run.

Despite adverse effects, toxic chemicals continue to be aggressively promoted by multinational companies attempting to expand their markets. These companies proclaim that agro-chemicals are essential to feed a hungry world. However, the evidence of the last 50 years shows that pesticides actually threaten global food security, diminish agricultural biodiversity and undermine long-term sustainability.

There already is a strong movement underway to

use more natural, sustainable methods for food production and pest management. In the United States alone, sales of organic products are growing at more than 20 percent per year. Farmers who are shifting from pesticides to using alternatives like crop rotation, natural predators and soil solarization, are finding a burgeoning market for their organic crops. They know they can produce flavorful, nutritious food and quality fiber while protecting the soil, air and water that we all depend on.

Organic farming is a big step toward a sustainable future. But we still have a long way to go.

Since we started our citizen's movement in 1982, Pesticide Action Network has evolved into an international network with regional centers on five continents. We link with partners—individuals, consumers, organic farmers, physicians, environ-mentalists, human rights activists, and farm labor groups—to educate and mobilize communities in over 60 countries.

Our solution is to advance pest management alternatives that are safer for our health, the health of generations to come, and the health of the planet.

Pesticide Action Network North America works with Regional Centers in Africa, Asia, Europe and Latin America. A few of our current campaigns include:

- *Fighting Hunger Without Pesticides.* We are raising our voices against a "New Green Revolution," which promotes intensive use of chemicals and genetically-engineered crops. We lobby development institutions including the World Bank, US AID and UN agencies to eliminate pesticide subsidies and support farmer-to-farmer education in natural management techniques — saving money, improving yields and returning control to local communities.

- *Preventing Export of Banned Pesticides.* As many food and clothing businesses in North America turn away from pesticides, multinational pesticide producers such as Dow, DuPont, Monsanto, Novartis, AgrEvo and Rhône-Poulenc are expanding their marketing in developing countries, who in turn export produce and fiber back to the countries where the pesticides were manufactured. We are collaborating with international partners to break this "Circle of Poison" and to strengthen pesticide regulation, trade restrictions and enforcement in Latin America and around the world.

- *Banning Methyl Bromide.* Pesticide Action Network supports and coordinates coalitions of consumers, farm workers and environmentalists to eliminate methyl bromide, a highly-toxic fumigant that depletes the earth's ozone layer. Methyl bromide has poisoned farmers and farmworkers, factory workers, school children and those who live near fields.

- *Promoting Our Right to Know.* We have a right to know about the poisons released into our environment. Pesticide Action Network gives citizens access to information about pesticide hazards and alternatives by publishing pesticide news, analyses and action alerts. We answer information requests from people around the world who have suffered pesticide poisonings and need emergency technical data or are looking for safe alternatives.

What can you do?

- Support the work of organizations like Pesticide Action Network by making a financial contribution.

- Buy certified organic, locally-grown produce and products made from organic fibers.

- Tell your legislators to press for stronger pesticide regulations and to halt the export of banned and unregistered pesticides.

- Educate your friends, neighbors and children about pesticides and alternatives.

- Question pesticide use and request information about pesticides used in your home, school, parks and workplace.

- Avoid using pesticides for household and garden pests-use healthy alternatives.

Food for All in the 21st Century

Rockefeller Foundation
420 Fifth Avenue
New York, NY 10018-2707
www.rockfund.org

Today, there are more than three-quarters of a billion people who live in a world where food is plentiful yet it is denied to them. According to recent estimates, over 800 million people, equivalent to 15% of the world's population, live a life of permanent or intermittent hunger and are chronically undernourished.

The first question we ought to ask ourselves is why should we be concerned?

We need to recognize that unless the developing countries are helped to realize sufficient food, employment and shelter for their growing population or to gain the means to purchase the food internally, the political stability of the world will be further undermined. In today's world, poverty and hunger, however remote, affect us all.

We have little time.

If nothing new is done, the numbers of poor and hungry will grow. By the year 2020, 21 years from now, there will be an extra two billion people in the developing world who will require food. This is additional to the three-quarters of a billion people who are chronically undernourished today.

What is the prognosis for feeding the world's population in the 21st Century?

It is not possible to foresee, with any accuracy, the situation in the later half of the next century. Predicting the next 21 years is more feasible, and this will be the most critical period; after 2020 the annual increments in the world population will begin to decrease significantly. If we can achieve a well-fed world by then, it should be possible to meet future demands, providing the resource base has been adequately protected.

If over the next two or three decades, we are to provide enough food for everyone we will have to:

• increase food production at a greater rate than in recent years, in a sustainable manner, without significantly damaging the environment and

• ensure it is accessible to all.

I believe these goals, when taken together, point to the need for a second Green Revolution. The new Green Revolution must not only benefit the poor more directly, but also must be applicable under highly diverse conditions and be environmentally sustainable. By implication, it must make greater use of indigenous resources, complemented by a far more judicious use of external inputs.

In effect, we require a Doubly Green Revolution, a revolution that is even more productive than the first Green Revolution and even more "Green" in terms of conserving natural resources and the environment.

I believe the challenge of the Doubly Green Revolution is only likely to be met by exploiting two key, recent developments in modern science: biotechnology and modern ecology.

Biotechnology, and especially genetic engineering, offers a faster route and also the means of tackling the particularly intractable problems of drought, salinity and toxicity that typically face the poorest farmers on the marginal lands.

One example of these benefits can be seen in efforts to improve rice varieties using these technologies. In 1984 the Rockefeller Foundation launched its International Program on Rice and Biotechnology to facilitate the creation of a number of Asian centers of excellence in biotechnology. To date over $80 million has been spent on collaborative programs with laboratories in the industrialized world. Practical results include the development, through tissue cultures, of a new rice variety in China, named *La Fen Rockefeller*, now widely grown in the Shanghai area and providing yields 25% above previous varieties. Genetically engineered rice is now available incorporating the *Bacillus thuringiensis* gene (Bt) which confers resistance to insect pests. Molecular markers have been used successfully to incorporate multiple resistance in rice in India, China and Columbia. Of even greater significance in the long term, rice is proving to be a model plant for cereal biotechnology. The major cereals have remarkably similar genomes and the techniques that have been acquired, and many of the genes themselves, have the capability of being utilized in wheat, maize, sorghum and millet breeding.

The potentials for genetic engineering are almost endless. But there are serious hazards. Perhaps the most obvious hazard is the possibility of a transferred gene being further passed through natural processes to another organism, with detrimental effects.

The developed countries are better equipped to access such hazards. They can call on a wide range of expertise and most have now set up regulatory bodies and are insisting on closely monitored trials to try and identify the likely risks before genetically engineered crops and livestock are released to the environment. So far, few developing countries have put such regulation in place, raising fears that developed country corporations may use developing country sites as unmonitored laboratories with potentially severe consequences.

My personal belief is that the hazards are often over-stated, but if the evident benefits are to be realized for the developing countries it is the responsibility of all involved to ensure the hazard assessments are as rigorous as in the developed countries.

More important than the potential hazards, at least to my mind, is the question of who benefits from genetic engineering, and indeed from conventional breeding processes. Genetic engineering is a highly competi-tive business and, inevitably, the focus of biotechnol-ogy companies has been on developed country mar-kets where potential sales are large. However biotech-nology companies are now turning their attention to the developing countries, and are embarking on an aggressive policy of identifying and patenting poten-tially useful genes. Part of the new answer to this chal-lenge lies in public-private partnerships where agree-ments ensure new varieties are freely available in the developing countries. But I believe that developing country governments and the international agricul-tural research institutes should also give priority to characterizing and patenting their own genetic mate-rials, to ensure they remain in the public domain.

The second development is the emergence of modern ecology, an equally powerful discipline, that is rapidly increasing our understanding of the structure and dynamics of agriculture and natural resources ecosystems and providing clues to their productive and sustainable management.

The widely successful application of Integrated Pest Management (IPM) to control rice pests in Southeast Asia is proof of what can be achieved. IPM looks at each crop and pest situation as a whole and then devises a program that integrates the various control methods in the light of all the factors present. The outcome is sustainable, efficient pest control that is often cheaper than the conventional use of pesticides.

A recent, highly successful example is IPM developed for both the brown planthopper and other rice pests in Indonesia. Under the program, farmers are trained to recognize and regularly monitor the pests and their natural enemies and use simple, yet effective rules to determine the minimum necessary use of pesticides. The outcome is a reduction in the average number of spraying from over four to less than one per season, while yields have grown from 6 to nearly 7.5 tons per hectare. Since 1986 rice production has increased 15% while pesticide use has declined to 60%, saving a $120 million per year in subsidies. The total economic benefit to 1990 was estimated to be over $1 billion. The farmer's health has improved and a, not insignificant, benefit has been the return of fish to the rice fields.

However, a successfully Doubly Green Revolution will not come from the application of biology alone. This new revolution has to reverse the chain of logic, starting with the socio-economic demands of poor households and then seeking to identify the appropriate research priorities.

Biologists will have to listen as well as instruct. There will be no easy solutions and few, if any, miracles in the new revolution. Greater food production will come from targeting local agro-ecosystems, making the most of indigenous resources, knowledge and analysis. More than ever before, we will have to forge genuine partnerships between biologists and farmers.

Over the past decade the development of powerful participatory techniques has produced a revolution every bit as important as the revolution in molecular and cellular biology and ecology. These new techniques are biotechnology, ecology and finally challenging the traditional top down process that has characterized so much development work. Participants from NGOs, Government agencies and the research centers rapidly find themselves, usually unexpectedly, listening as much as talking, experiencing close to first hand the conditions of life in poor households and changing their perceptions about the kinds of interventions and the research needs that are required.

If we can bring all three together, I believe we can feed the world in a way that is not only equitable but also sustainable.

Healthy Soil, Food, and People

Rodale Institute

611 Siegfridale Road
Kutztown, PA 19530
✽

M aking the vital connection between healthy soil and healthy people—the basis of sustainable cuisine—has been the central thrust of the Rodale Institute for more than three generations.

Rodale Institute was the brainchild of J.I. Rodale who moved to rural Pennsylvania in the late 1930s where he was able to realize his keen personal interest in farming. Developing and demonstrating practical methods of rebuilding natural soil fertility became J.I. Rodale's primary goal when a shortage of nitrogen during World War II—diverted from fertilizers to munitions—exposed the natural nutrient poverty of the nation's soil.

In 1947, J.I. founded the Soil and Health Foundation, the forerunner of Rodale Institute. He also created publications including *Health Bulletin, Organic*

Farming and Gardening and *Prevention Magazine* and formed his central message and philosophy: Healthy Soil = Healthy Food = Healthy People.

The concept was simple but it was also revolutionary.

While widely accepted a century ago, chemical fertilizers, pesticides, herbicides, hormones, artificial ingredients, preservatives, and additives for taste and appearance had changed the face of agriculture. As J.I. Rodale communicated the idea of creating soil rich in nutrients and free of contaminants, however, people began to listen and acceptance grew. "Organics is not a fad," J.I. wrote in 1954. "It has been a long-established practice—much more firmly grounded than the current chemical flair. Present agriculture practices are leading us downhill."

Today the Rodale Institute continues to complete groundbreaking research at its Experimental Farm, working to study, prove and communicate the soil health-human health connection.

Rodale-style farming has changed over the years— from organic to low-input to sustainable to regenerative—but the intent is unchanged: to provide more healthful food by creating and maintaining healthy soil.

Central to the success of the Institute are its goals. We believe these goals are important to the concept of sustainable cuisine:

• To help people rediscover that the food they eat is a primary tool in achieving optimum health and avoiding illness and disease.

• To reach out to young people and become partners in reshaping public attitudes.

• To make soil quality as important to the public as air and water quality.

• To encourage more people to grow, sell, and buy organic food.

• To build consumer demand for food grown by regenerative and organic farmers.

• To include regenerative farmers, food companies and food stores on the same team as medical and other health-care professionals.

• To respect and interpret that the mind and soul require nourishment as part of total human health and a regenerative way of life.

To meet these goals, the Rodale Institute Experimental Farm, stresses five research initiatives: 1) Soil health, 2) Food quality, 3) Food systems education, 4) Composting, 5) Community development.

Long the site of important farming systems trial, The Experimental Farm is now increasing its emphasis on education. It forges new collaborations and partnerships, and communicates its results and their clear implications to the public, especially young people and decision-makers in the food industry. In addition, the Rodale Institute works with food industry leaders to show them how to adopt more healthful methods and still prosper.

<hr />

Sustainable, the Second Time Around

Marcus Fruchter

Second Harvest
116 South Michigan Avenue, Suite 4
Chicago, Illinois 60603-6001
www.secondharvest.org

Second Harvest is the largest hunger-relief organization in the United States. Our mission is to feed hungry people by soliciting and distributing food and grocery products through a nationwide network of certified affiliate food banks and to educate the public about the nature of hunger in America. Our network serves all 50 states and Puerto Rico by distributing food and grocery products to more than 46,000 local charitable hunger-relief agencies, including food pantries, soup kitchens, women's shelters, Kids Cafes, and other organizations that provide emergency food assistance. Last year, Second Harvest distributed one billion pounds of food and grocery products, providing emergency food assistance to more than 26 million hungry Americans, including eight million children and four million seniors.

Hunger in the United States is a consequence of poverty. Although hunger and poverty are inextricably linked as public policy problems, the problem of hunger can be solved even if the larger issue of poverty is not or cannot. We strongly believe that hunger in America is completely curable. The "prescription for the cure" requires an innovative partnership of the public and private sectors aimed at creating a seamless safety net for low-income people.

Sustainable cuisine can be an important part of this partnership. The concept has the potential to bring farmers, food processors, the retail food industry, environmentalists and charitable organizations together to develop and promote behaviors that produce and distribute food in ways that are environmentally and socially responsible. We encourage restaurants, grocery stores, grocery product manufacturers, and most importantly, consumers, to employ the concepts of sustainable cuisine to help feed and sustain the approximately 35 million men, women and children who are hungry each day in our nation.

It is fitting that this Sustainable Cuisine Dinner is devoted to exploring and discussing ways to sustain and preserve the earth and its inhabitants in future centuries and for future generations.

∽∾∽

Sharing
Our Strength

Share Our Strength

733 15th Street, NW, Suite 640
Washington, DC 20005
www.strength.org
~✿

Share Our Strength, a national anti-hunger and anti-poverty organization, has mobilized a network of thousands of chefs all over the country to join the fight against hunger by volunteering their time and expertise to raise money for anti-hunger efforts. Since its inception in 1984, Share Our Strength has raised and distributed more than $50 million to over 1,000 anti-hunger programs.

Operation Frontline, a program of Share Our Strength, takes chefs' involvement beyond fundraising. Participating chefs volunteer their time to share their cooking skills, their creativity and their passion for good food with people who struggle to feed their families on limited incomes.

Since its inception in 1993, more than 11,000 people have participated in Operation Frontline classes and over 21,000 have received nutrition information through nutrition fairs and related events. Operation Frontline classes are currently running in over 80 communities in 12 states.

Operation Frontline works in collaboration with local community-based non-profit organizations. Project Place, a community agency in Boston, MA, is one example. A recent evaluation of a job training program they run revealed that poor health was one of the major roadblocks to success in the workplace for many of the program's participants. Project Place was able to address this need by offering a six-week Operation Frontline class to the programs participants.

Project Place's program director Sharon Carey wrote to us about the impact of the cooking class:

> "...You and your chefs convinced us that nutritious eating leads to good health and showed how this can be accomplished on a very modest budget. You challenged us to examine lifestyles and make changes where appropriate. You provided new choices. It was obvious from people's conversations and questions at the end of the class, that they have acquired useful, new information and are now more keenly aware of the connection between good eating and good health. Old habits die hard, but I know from working and eating with our students every day, positive change has begun and I believe will continue.
>
> People are also thinking more critically about how foods are advertised. Students admitted that they pretty much believed what promoters said about a product and were stunned to discover that what they heard on TV, or read in print, was often not the

whole truth. They enjoyed the trip to Wollaston's market were they learned about unit pricing and marketing from Frank Miller, and realized that they had to become their own investigators. The students talked about how they were now less likely to be manipulated by slick promotions.

The students loved working together in the kitchen. Many said that one of the hardest things about being homeless and living in a shelter, is that you never get to cook for yourself or your family. I'll never forget when Theresa said, 'I had forgotten how wonderful cooking smells are...better than perfume!' Everyone agreed. What wonderful therapy to chop and stir and share stories with a group while perfecting new skills and working towards a common goal.

Soon after Operation Frontline classes ended, we were scheduled to feed seventy-five people at our annual Thanksgiving Day Feast. At eight that morning our cook got sick and left work. There was a minute of horrible panic and then the Operation Frontline graduates took charge. They rolled up their sleeves, washed their hands in warm, soapy water and went to work. They proved to be a great team; with skill and confidence they served a wonderful, healthy (except for the pie table) meal to a crowd of people and had a great time doing it."

Operation Frontline is an anti-hunger program that celebrates the pleasures of good food while providing essential cooking, nutrition and food budgeting information. This is our example of sustainable cuisine.

Slow is Sustainable

Patrick Martins

Slow Food
Via della Mendicita Istruita, 8
12042 Bra (CN) Italy
www.slowfood.com

ॱॱ

In August 1998, I began working at the International Offices of the Slow Food Movement located in Bra, Italy, and became Director of the Movement in the US and Canada in December 1998 (a Slow Food national office based out of New York City is being planned for November of 1999).

The Slow Food Movement is a non-profit organization founded in the Piedmont region of Italy by Carlo Petrini in 1986. Our goal is to promote mankind's inalienable right to pleasure through good eating and counter the onslaught of fast-food and supermarket culture that standardize tastes and extinguish local variety in the production of food and beverages. In order to eat well, we believe it is necessary to reawaken and save "slow" or sustainable local cooking traditions, a lost ethic in an age when technology and speed have come to effect the way we eat (hence the snail logo).

We also hope to create a network to provide a voice for small food and beverage producers. The Movement achieved international status in 1989 when delegates from 20 countries met in Paris to sign the official Slow Food Manifesto. Today, Slow Food has over 60,000 members in 35 countries who delight in their particular gastronomic heritage or want to learn about others.

The Slow Food Movement goes about saving the world's quality food and beverage heritage in three ways. The first is our Ark Project that is a scientific and advertising strategy that documents and protects food and drinks in danger of extinction. Our hope is that increased visibility of these products will convince consumers to seek them out and restaurants to serve them so that market demand will spur supply. Many of our Ark products have been nominated to be exceptions to the often oppressive European Union regulations that hurt small food producers. An extension of the Ark Project is a program being developed by Slow Food called Food Garrisons. These garrisons are pieces of land operated by Slow Food to make the Ark Project active. For instance, planting and making wines that are not made anymore and raising animal species that are no longer raised because of high costs are some ideas in the works.

Another project is our taste education program. This program gets implemented through our 475 Convivia (chapters) in 35 countries that put on monthly food events for members. Our major gastronomic events like the Salone del Gusto (with 3,000 wines from around the world and over 350 taste workshops, this event, which is held every two years, includes gastronomic products such as cheeses, cold meats, olive oils, vinegars, breads, chocolates, and liqueurs from 30 countries—the event attracted 126,000 visitors in 1998); Cheese (the largest cheese event in the world held every two years which boasted all cheeses of denomination of protected origin in Europe in 1997); the Three Glass Presentation (a yearly event in New York which allows attendees to taste the best Italian wines); and through our publications, which include a quarterly journal and various books including *Doing, Saying Tasting: Taste Education in Grade Schools*.

Our final project is Fraternal Tables, which involves donations to feed those who need assistance. We currently have three active tables: one in Brazil, one in Sarajevo, and one in Italy. One of the stipulations for these donations is that proceeds feed victims of manmade and natural disasters.

Through these three projects, Slow Food hopes to accumulate a network of quality producers, Convivia, and members and restaurants that buy from them. By promoting and supporting these foods and drinks in various ways, Slow Food hopes to celebrate biodiversity and defend sustainable cuisine (what we call our food and beverage heritage). The need for sustainable cuisine is obvious: it is a part of who we are. Protecting food traditions is no less important than protecting species of animals, preserving churches, castles and cathedrals or collecting objects in a museum. It is obvious that slow eating is not always possible in this day and age but eating well should also be made a priority. Eating well implies conviviality, sitting at a table with family or friends, interesting conversation, and rediscovering the flavours and savors of regional cooking.

Through our journal, events, and projects the Slow Food Movement hopes that food related issues like sustainable cuisine will become a discourse that gets talked about regularly from dinner tables to the halls of government. We also hope that being ready to pay more for quality (since many small producers cannot compete with the price slashing tactics of big industry), seeking out quality products, and respecting the natural rhythms of mankind when eating will be natural next steps to thinking about sustainable cuisine. I will finish this letter with our Slow Food Manifesto which excellently conveys the humor and seriousness of what the Slow Food Movement is about.

The Slow Food Manifesto

This document was approved at the Founding conference of the Slow Food Movement Paris, December 9, 1989.

Our century, which began and has developed under the insignia of industrial civilization, first invented the machine and then took it as its life model. We are enslaved by speed and have all succumbed to the same insidious virus: Fast Life, which disrupts our habits, pervades the privacy of our homes and forces us to eat Fast Foods. To be worthy of the name, Homo Sapiens should rid himself of speed before it reduces him to a species in danger of extinction. A firm defense of quiet material pleasure is the only way to oppose the universal folly of Fast Life. May suitable doses of guaranteed sensual pleasure and slow, long lasting enjoyment preserve us from the contagion of the multitude that mistaken frenzy for efficiency. Our defense should begin at the table with Slow Food. Let us rediscover the flavors and savors of regional cooking and banish the degrading effects of Fast Food. In the name of productivity, Fast Life has changed our way of being and threatens our environment and our landscapes. So Slow Food is now the only truly progressive answer. That is what real culture is all about: developing taste rather than demeaning it. And what better way to set about this than an international exchange of experiences, knowledge, projects? Slow Food guarantees a better future. Slow Food is an idea that needs plenty of qualified supporters who can help turn this (slow) motion into an international movement, with the little snail as its symbol.

⸙

Sustainable Cuisine:
A Word from
the Galley

Michael Romano, Chef

Union Square Cafe
21 East 16th Street
New York, NY 10003
❧

My definition of sustainable cuisine is rather simple. Sustainable cuisine means nurturing that which nurtures us.

As a chef, the second from the last stop in a rather lengthy food chain that starts with seeds in soil (the last, of course, being the customer), I find the concept of sustainable cuisine imminently logical. As the only element in the food consumption chain with the ability to discern and choose, human beings must recognize that it is our environment that grants us life, gives us sustenance and continues to provide for our nourishment.

We've all been told that for every reaction there is an equal reaction, a consequence, an effect, and sustainable cuisine is no exception.

Recently the Federal Government sought protection for nine wild salmon species in the Pacific Northwest, under the provisions of the Endangered Species Act. It was an effort applauded by environmentalists and for good reason—protecting our natural resources, such as salmon, is important. But there's another side of the story. People will be affected. Their taxes may increase to purchase land around the waterways. They may face building restrictions and other changes to their lifestyles. One good idea—protecting species—suddenly gets a little more complicated.

Inevitably we ask ourselves how willing are we to change our lives for important concepts such as sustainable cuisine? How far will we go?

A while back I addressed this issue as a chef and a concerned citizen. I decided that I would attempt to buy organic, local, in-season goods for our restaurant. While there have been practical compromises along the way, we strive toward that goal and have been fairly successful achieving it.

We've been able to work with the food growers at our local farmers' market and as a result Union Square diners have enjoyed the freshest possible corn, asparagus, berries, stone fruits and okra on their plates. And while the reality is that some foods have a year-round place on our menu—such as egg-plant, peppers, artichokes and fennel—we try to be very aware of how and where the food we serve was grown. We forbid berries from South America and Mexico because it is understood that pesticides were used in their cultivation. We also try to be sensitive to the issue of transportation—favoring locally grown food rather than items that consume excess fossil fuels as they are trucked to our restaurant.

It wasn't too long ago in New York City that running a luxurious restaurant meant you could get "any food, any time of the year"—strawberries in January if you wanted! Now there is greater awareness among chefs and customers that you shouldn't get strawberries in January because there is a logic and a grace to following the seasons.

Instead, we investigate what's in season by talking to the farmers that come to sell their products in the local farmers' market. We invite farmers in to talk about what and how they are growing or producing food. They meet our patrons. I visit their farms. We trek down to the market to see, touch and smell their fresh goods. Regular visits to the farmers' market has become part of who we are and what we do. And the farmers we have visited for years are starting to prosper. Guy Jones, for example, a regular at the Union Square Greenmarket, has become very popular and has a steady flow of chefs who stop by, hang out and share knowledge—an age old village tradition alive and well right here on 14th Street.

Our efforts, along with those of the Chef's Collaborative 2000, a group of chefs who are thinking about sustainability, are creating a quiet shift in consciousness. Cooking schools are now starting to take note and there's hope that the next generation of chefs will carry on our efforts. I do wish that restaurant reviewers would take greater note of this important trend. They should react to the fact that a restaurant is serving asparagus in December and applaud those restaurants that make the effort to serve more seasonal produce.

The ultimate taste test for sustainable cuisine is the tabletop. The biggest factor that influences the taste of food is freshness. The fresher the food, the more that food retains the intensity of its flavor. While there are compromises along the way, the proof of sustainable cuisine is as simple as a bowl of ripe strawberries, a bushel of New Jersey tomatoes in season, and a bounty of fresh okra, carrots and broccoli.

Save Money,
Save Time,
Save the Planet

David Garza

Urban Organic
230 A 7th Street
Brooklyn, NY 11215
www.urbanorganic.com

❧

Urban Organic was founded to create widespread availability of organic, sustainable cuisine, to all members of the community at affordable prices. The entire existence of our company is based on the importance of organic food to the health of our people and the protection of the environment. In essence, sustainable cuisine is our business and my life's work. After graduating Harvard in 1986 and spending years in retail management working for Macy's and The Gap, I became involved with Urban Organic through a partnership opportunity with a childhood friend. Together, we believe we can make an impact on the business world and help the global community at the same time.

Why is "sustainable cuisine" important to us?

- *It protects the environment.* When you purchase organic food, you use the power of your dollar to sustain life affirming farming practices.

- *You also get better flavor.* There is a good reason why many chefs use organic food in their recipes— it tastes better! Organic farming starts with the nourishment of the soil, which leads to the nourishment of the plant and, ultimately, our palates.

- *It protects our children.* The average child is exposed to four times as many cancer-causing pesticides in their food than an adult. Organic food contains no carcinogenic pesticides.

- *It prevents soil erosion.* The Soil Conservation Society estimates that more than 3 billion tons of topsoil are eroded from United States farmlands each year, and soil is eroding seven times faster than it is being built up naturally. In organic farming, soil is the foundation of the food chain as opposed to conventional farming where soil is merely used as a method of holding the plants in place so they can be chemically fertilized.

- *It protects water quality.* Water makes up two-thirds of the planet's mass. The Environmental Protection Agency estimates pesticides contaminate the groundwater in 38 states, polluting the primary source of water for more than half the country's population.

- *It saves energy.* Farming methods have changed drastically in this century from small family farms to large-scale factory style farms dependent upon fossil fuels. Modern farming uses more petroleum than any other single industry.

- *It keeps chemicals off your plate.* The FDA approved many pesticides before research linked them to chemicals that cause cancer and other diseases. Now the EPA considers 60% of all herbicides, 90% of all fungicides, and 30% of all insecticides to be carcinogenic. The bottom line is that pesticides are poisons made to kill living creatures and can also be harmful to humans.

- *It protects farm workers' health.* A National Cancer Institute study showed that farmers exposed to chemical herbicides had a six times greater risk of contracting cancer than farmers who are not exposed. The health of farm workers in developing countries is a serious issue, as pesticide use is poorly regulated. An estimated 1 million people are poisoned annually by pesticides, and in developing countries 25 million farm workers suffer acute pesticide poisoning every year.

- *It helps small farmers.* Most organic farms are independently owned and operated family farms. It is estimated that the United States has lost more than 650,000 family farms in the past decade.

- *It supports a true economy.* Superficially, organic foods might seem more expensive than conventional foods. Conventional food prices do not reflect hidden costs borne by the taxpayer, including nearly $74 billion in federal subsidies to conventional farming in 1988. Other hidden costs include pesticide regulation and testing, hazardous waste disposal, and environmental damage. A recent study by Cornell University concluded that pesticides cost our nation $8 billion annually. Soil erosion cost another $24 billion.

- *It promotes bio-diversity.* "Mono-cropping" is the practice of planting large lots of land with the same crop year after year; conventional farming uses this method exclusively. The lack of natural diversity of plant life has left the soil lacking in natural nutrients and minerals. To replace these lost nutrients which are necessary to farm, chemical fertilizers are often used. Single crops are also much more susceptible to pests, making farmers even more reliant on pesticides.

Organic farming encourages food production that nurtures our soil through the absence of pesticides and the presence of rich compost. The inherent commitment of organic farming to crop rotation, living soil, rural enterprise, pure water and sustainable agriculture is, in itself, a critical step toward protecting our environment and our individual health. By buying organic, you provide a marketplace for growers who have made the future of our planet a top priority.

What A Long Important Trip It Is...

Robert Weir

Guitarist/Singer
The Grateful Dead

❧

Music and cooking are very similar. They're all about blending and all about taste.

I always enjoyed cooking since I was a kid. At 16, Jerry Garcia, Pigpen and myself started a band that went on to become The Grateful Dead. For years the band has taken up the cause to protect and preserve the environment.

Environmental activism has been a long time passion with me. The degradation of the environment made me realize that I couldn't just sit back. I have tried to share my passion with my fans to swell the ranks of environmentalism.

Sustainable cuisine is the natural evolution of the environmental movement. The Grateful Dead have always been about the adventures of the soul. Clearly, sustainable cuisine can carry us to new places that are satisfying, healthy and, above all, sustainable.

Music and food delight and nourish the spirit!

Enchante, peace and veggies.

Selling Sustainable Cuisine

Whole Foods Market

Corporate Office
601 North Lamar, Suite 300
Austin, TX 78703
www.wholefoods.com

᠅

Whole Foods Market is the largest purveyor of Natural Foods in the world. We're like an old-fashioned neighborhood grocery store, an organic farmers' market, a European bakery, a New York deli, and a modern supermarket all rolled into one!

Our company's mission is very consistent with the principles of sustainable cuisine. In fact, our mission and motto—Whole Foods, Whole People, Whole Planet—reflects our awareness and respect for the interdependence that exists between us, our customers and our communities.

We appreciate and celebrate that great food and cooking improves the lives of all of our stakeholders.

Breaking bread with each other, eating healthfully and eating well—these are some of the great joys of our lives.

We see the necessity of active environmental steward-ship so that the earth continues to flourish for gener-ations to come. We seek to balance our needs with the needs of the rest of the planet through several actions:

- Supporting sustainable agriculture. We are com-mitted to greater production of organically and biodynamically grown foods in order to reduce pesticide use and promote soil conservation.

- Reducing waste and consumption of non-renew-able resources. We promote and participate in recycling programs in our communities. We are committed to re-usable packaging, reducing pack-aging, and water and energy conservation.

- Encouraging environmentally sound cleaning and store maintenance programs.

Our core values define our approach to sustainable cuisine. These are not values that change from time to time, situation to situation, or person to person, but rather they are the underpinning of our company culture. Many people feel Whole Foods is an exciting company of which to be a part and a very special place to work. These core values are the primary rea-sons for this feeling, and they transcend our size and our growth rate. By maintaining these core values, regardless of how large a company Whole Foods becomes, we can preserve what has always been special about our company. These core values are the soul of our company and they help us promote the concept of sustainable cuisine in our stores everyday:

- We appreciate and celebrate the difference natural and organic products can make in the quality of one's life.

- We have high standards and our goal is to sell the highest quality products we possibly can. We define quality by evaluating the ingredients, freshness, safety, taste, nutritive value and appearance of all of the products we carry. We are buying agents for our customers and not the selling agents for the manufacturers.

- Our customers are the most important stakeholders in our business and the lifeblood of our business. Only by satisfying our customers first do we have the opportunity to satisfy the needs of our other stakeholders.

- We can generate greater appreciation and loyalty from all of our stakeholders by educating them about natural and organic foods, health, nutrition and the environment.

- We support organic farmers, growers and the environment through our commitment to sustainable agriculture and by expanding the market for organic products.

- We respect our environment and recycle, reuse, and reduce our waste wherever and whenever we can.

- We recognize our responsibility to be active participants in our local communities. We give a minimum of 5% of our profits every year to a wide variety of community and non-profit organizations. In addition, we pay our Team Members to give of their time to community and service organizations.

Toward a Truly Sustainable Cuisine

Ismail Serageldin

Chairman
Consultative Group on International
Agricultural Research (CGIAR)

Vice President, Special Programs
The World Bank

T he very word "cuisine" has a beautiful ring to it, calling up memories or, perhaps, hopes of exotic gastronomic delights. But what we are talking about here is not just cuisine—"a style of preparing food" *(Webster)*—but of the whole process from pre-production through growth and harvesting to post-production and consumption. We are talking about the need to ensure that at each of the steps along the way, food abundance and environmental conservation go hand-in-hand. This is an important, indeed, crucial commitment.

For millions across our planet, however, styles of cooking are distant luxuries. Access to food is their daily challenge. The challenge grows more acute, under the pressures of population growth and environmental degradation. It is particularly timely, therefore, that the world should shake itself out of any feelings of complacency towards the issue of food security. It is fundamentally important that the world reassess the prospects for achieving food security for all, and abolish the scandal of hunger in a world of plenty, as we enter the third millennium.

To do so, all of us who care about our fellow human beings must be motivated by a sense of outrage, and they must understand the stakes correctly, and be appropriately informed about the issues in order to respond with the right actions.

It is inconceivable that there should be some 800 million persons going hungry in a world that can provide for that most basic of all human needs. In the last century, some people looked at the condition of slavery and said that it was monstrous and unconscionable. That it must be abolished. They were known as the abolitionists. They did not argue from economic self-interest, but from moral outrage. Today the condition of hunger in a world of plenty is equally monstrous and unconscionable and must be abolished. We must become the "New Abolitionists". We must, with the same zeal and moral outrage, attack the complacency that would turn a blind eye to this silent holocaust which claims some 40,000 hunger-related deaths every day.

The stakes ahead are enormous, and agricultural research stands at the heart of it. For agriculture is not only the means of producing food for the billions of humans on the planet, it is the key interface between humans and the natural environment. In the developing countries, where 80% of the population live, agriculture accounts for about 70% of the land used, and 80% of the water. If agriculture is not intensified, in an environmentally appropriate fashion, the sheer expansion of the population and its requirements will lead to the destruction of the forests from slash and burn farming of poor, small holders who eke out a meager living. The hillsides will be further colonized and the soil further degraded and eroded. More water will be lost, and more will go hungry as they become environmental refugees. This will be our legacy if we do not transform agriculture.

Transforming agriculture, however, is just a small part of the overall equation. It must be done in a manner that benefits, even relies on, the small holder farmers of the developing world. That will reduce rural poverty, reduce vulnerability, and improve food security. Cheap food will also be critical as the single most direct and effective program for assisting the urban poor who have to purchase their food.

The transformation of agriculture is not going to happen without a sustained and continuing investment in agricultural research at the international and the national level. The private sector will not undertake some of the critical research essential to the promotion of sustainable agriculture for food security in the developing countries, because so much of it is of a public goods nature. That is why the Consultative Group on International Agricultural Research (CGIAR) and national institutes in the developing countries must receive even greater support.

Beyond the production side is the access side. Special efforts to reduce poverty among the poorest of the poor remains absolutely essential, and access to resources is fundamental to improving their status. This is where the experience of micro-finance becomes so important. It is a means of promoting access, solidarity and reducing vulnerability among the very poor. The Consultative Group to Assist the Poorest (CGAP) and similar instruments become essential tools to attack this problem.

Thus food security is not just about production, it is very much about poverty and this diagnosis is essential to adopting the right responses: agricultural research, access to credit, promotion of sustainable agriculture with special focus on the small-holder farmers, and above all an unremitting battle against poverty. These are the directions to be pursued. The logic of the policies and programs must be matched by determined implementation. It is here that the sense of outrage must assert itself, if we are to truly act as the "new abolitionists".

The world will then be able to think in terms of a new and shared abundance in which cuisine becomes truly sustainable.

ACKNOWLEDGEMENTS

Careers Through Culinary Arts Program
Service
(212) 873-2434

Cabbage Hill Farm Foundation
Greens
(914) 241-2774
www.cabbagehillfarm.org

Cascadian Farm
Dairy
(360) 855-0100
www.cfarm.com

Chartrand Imports
Wine
(800) 473-7307
www.midcoast.com/~chartran

Chefwear
Chef Coats
800-568-2433
www.chefwear.com

D'Artagnan, Inc.
Quail
(800) DARTAGN
www.dartagnan.com

Egg Farm Dairy
Dairy
(800) 273-2637
(800) CREAMERY
www.eggfarmdairy.com

Elysian Farms
Lamb
724-852-1076

Equal Exchange
Coffee
(781) 830-0303
www.equalexchange.com

Fantastic Foods
Rice
(707) 778-7801
www.fantasticfoods.com

Fresh Tech Inc.
Refrigerator Freshners
(203) 618-0268
jefreshtch@aol.com

gepa 3 The Fair Trade Company
Organic Tea
(212) 529-5787
www.gepa3.com

Green Field Paper Company
Grow-a-note/flowers and herbs
(619) 338-9432
www.greenfieldpaper.com

Greenmarket Farmers Market
Decoration
(212) 477-3220

Gmund
Coasters
(404) 943-1255

Interface, Inc.
Floorcovering and Service Provider
(770)-437-6800
www.interfaceinc.com

Keeper Springs Mountain Spring Water
Bottled Water
(212) 343-9945
www.keepersprings.com

Martinelli's
Apple Juice and Cider
(800) 662-1868
www.martinellis.com

Metropolis Magazine
Magazines
(212) 627-9977
www.metropolismagazine.com

The New York Botanical Garden
Passes
(718) 817-8700
www.nybg.org

Paul Newman/Newman's Own

OCP Chocolate (Organic Commodity Products)
Chocolate (baking and bars)
(617) 661-1100
ocp@shore.net

Organic Valley
Dairy
(608) 625-2602
www.organicvalley.com

Organic Wine Company
Wine
(888) ECO-WINE
www.ecowine.org

Petaluma Poultry (Rocky Chicken)
Poultry
(707) 763-1904

Rainbow Eco Specialties
Mugs
(800) 842-0527
www.ecospec.com

Skipper Seafood, Certified Turtle Safe Shrimp
Shrimp
912-437-4046

Smucker Quality Beverages
Santa Cruz Organic
R.W. Knudsen Family
Juices and Cider
(530) 899-5000
www.jmsmucker.com

Stonyfield Farm
Yogurt
(603) 437-4040
www.stonyfield.com

SWG Enterprises Inc.
Cooking Equipment
(818) 881-4586

Tom's of Maine
Toothpaste
(207)985-2944
www.toms-of-maine.com

Urban Organic
Produce and Bags
(718) 499-4321
www.urbanorganic.com

Whole Foods Market
Pasta
(512) 477-5566
www.wholefoods.com

Wolaver's Certified Organic Ales
Beer
(888) 595-BREW
www.wolavers.com

ZAGAT Survey
Restaurant Guides
800-333-3421
www.zagat.com